REPORTS!
FORMATTING
APPLICATIONS

SECOND EDITION

GEORGE P. GRILL

Information Systems &
Operations Management
Department

University of North Carolina
Greensboro, North Carolina

AF326970

TA06BA
PUBLISHED BY
SOUTH-WESTERN PUBLISHING CO.
CINCINNATI, OH   WEST CHICAGO, IL   DALLAS, TX   LIVERMORE, CA

Copyright © 1990

by SOUTH-WESTERN PUBLISHING CO.

Cincinnati, Ohio

ISBN: 0-538-60167-1

Library of Congress Catalog Card Number: 89-62836

2 3 4 5 6 7 8 K 6 5 4 3 2 1 0

Printed in the United States of America

Preface

The overall objective of REPORTS! FORMATTING APPLICATIONS is to provide an intensive review for formatting/keyboarding a variety of reports. To accomplish this objective, this book systematically introduces the different types of reports as they are needed for personal, business, and professional use. The five primary objectives are as follows: (1) to review different formats of reports; (2) to present layout guides for formatting/keyboarding reports; (3) to provide a variety of complex problems, ranging from the simple to the complex; (4) to handle realistic problems from rough draft, script, and corrected script; and (5) to develop word processing marketable skills and self-confidence in formatting and keyboarding reports.

REPORTS! FORMATTING APPLICATIONS may be used by readers with no previous formatting background. It has been specifically designed for use in all kinds of keyboarding courses on the secondary and postsecondary levels, including word processing courses, personal keyboarding courses, and managerial training courses for office systems workers.

REPORTS! FORMATTING APPLICATIONS provides readers with step-by-step introductions to formatting reports. Each type of report is thoroughly explained and illustrated with examples. This book is segmented into two parts. Part One, Reports for Personal Use, contains an introduction to themes; book reviews; unbound reports with reference citations; top-bound reports with reference citations and title pages; leftbound reports with citations and title pages; reports with outlines, footnotes, and bibliography; and reference sections on proofreader's marks and editing functions. Part Two, Reports for Business and Professional Use, incorporates short, informal business reports; simplified memorandum reports; traditional memorandum reports; documented business reports; professional journal articles; minutes of meetings; and news releases.

Each part is divided into sections that include (1) background information, (2) layout guides, (3) models, and (4) jobs in rough draft, script, and corrected script copy. Directions for keyboarding jobs are included. Editing functions will be suggested (the first time they are used) for those students using a word processor. Students are then expected to use editing functions as needed. Students are also instructed to proofread, correct all errors, and produce a final corrected report.

Many individuals have assisted me in the preparation of REPORTS! FORMATTING APPLICATIONS. My sincerest thanks to these individuals who permitted me to include their ideas and words. I wish to acknowledge their support and encouragement.

George P. Grill

Contents

Reports are tools used by management of a business and by instructors of an educational institution to provide meaningful information. Reports may be for personal use or for professional and business use. They may be short or long and prepared in different formats.

In Sections A and B, you will key themes and book reviews, which are typical of informal school reports. In the remaining sections of Part One, you will key reports that are more formal and that have been researched. The contents of these reports contain factual data. You will learn how to key unbound, topbound, and leftbound reports. You will also learn to key outlines, title pages, reference citations, footnotes, and bibliographies. If using a word processor, use the editing functions (see page 47).

Section A   THEMES

A theme is a short and accurate description of ideas on a particular topic. To compose an effective theme, limit the subject matter to that which adequately covers the topic. After analyzing the subject and gathering data, list the major ideas in outline form. An outline makes it easier to develop meaningful topic sentences and to arrange the subject matter into related paragraphs which support topic sentences.

Since keyboarding is much faster than handwriting, develop the habit of using a typewriter or word processor to compose your thoughts. Use proofreader's marks (see page 46) to correct the first draft; then retype it or revise it as the final copy. Proofread and correct all errors before removing your paper or printing a final copy. If using a word processor, use editing functions (see page 47).

Layout Guides

The themes in Section A are to be formatted from the model, rough draft, script, and corrected script. The following guides represent one acceptable form for formatting themes:

1. Margins: Top margin, first page, is 9 blank lines for pica and 11 blank lines for elite type. Side margins are 1". Bottom margin is at least 1" (6 blank lines).
2. DS (double-space) the text; indent first line of paragraphs 5 spaces.
3. Center title in ALL CAPS (space: 42, pica; 51, elite).
4. QS (quadruple-space) below title to body of report.
5. For second and subsequent pages, key the page number on line 6 at right margin and continue keying the theme on line 8.

Main Heading   WORD PROCESSING CONCEPTS   line 10, pica

QS

The business office structure is changing to a word processing environment. It involves a change in equipment and structure, a change of roles and responsibilities for employees, and a change of terminology.

Changes in business are not always gradual; this one came fast and full-scale. Within a few months, many businesses have gone from a traditional office structure to a full-fledged word processing structure. Why? Money! Control of expenses!

In its simplest form, word processing is the transition of ideas in your head to a typewritten form that is readable and understandable by others. It is a composite of ideas, people, procedures, equipment, and environment which makes up the organization's total communication system. The concept of word processing is the redefining of jobs, the restructuring of procedures, the redistribution of people to handle specialized work, and the automated, cost-controlled approach to some familiar office routines.

The goals of word processing in the business office are to control expenses, to increase productivity, and to develop efficient administrative procedures by using existing resources. People in offices will need to understand more about modern office methods and functions, to acquire new office skills, and to learn to work in environments that use sophisticated office equipment and procedures.

(at least 1")

Main Heading WORD PROCESSING CONCEPTS   line 12, elite

QS

The business office structure is changing to a word processing environment. It involves a change in equipment and structure, a change of roles and responsibilities for employees, and a change of terminology.

Changes in business are not always gradual; this one came fast and full-scale. Within a few months, many businesses have gone from a traditional office structure to a full-fledged word processing structure. Why? Money! Control of expenses!

In its simplest form, word processing is the transition of ideas in your head to a typewritten form that is readable and understandable by others. It is a composite of ideas, people, procedures, equipment, and environment which makes up the organization's total communication system. The concept of word processing is the redefining of jobs, the restructuring of procedures, the redistribution of people to handle specialized work, and the automated, cost-controlled approach to some familiar office routines.

The goals of word processing in the business office are to control expenses, to increase productivity, and to develop efficient administrative procedures by using existing resources. People in offices will need to understand more about modern office methods and functions, to acquire new office skills, and to learn to work in environments that use sophisticated office equipment and procedures.

(at least 1")

Marcumm said that the titles of the operas for 1990 season will be announced at the next meeting.

2

The company must plan two years in advance because of the need to sign artists well ahead of their actual appearance here.

~~This year's opera budget will increase to approximately $250,000,~~ ~~Also,~~ an extensive opera education program is under way in the nearby communities.

Guest artist Elana McCarley, who sang excerpts from "La Boheme" Monday evening, is touring city and county schools with the program. The city school program this year features visits by docents from the company. Mark Carpenter, *director* ~~head~~ of the education committee, said the culmination of the education program this year will be a March presentation of "Cinderella" and "Don Pasquale" for fifth, sixth, and seventh graders. The education program is supported by a grant from the Crawford Foundation.

New board members are Jane Curtis, Ann York, Philip Jenkins, Ruth Beaman, Philip Zinnser, Albert Chung, and Carmen Torres.

The ~~annual~~ meeting was held Tuesday, October 15, at the United Presbyterian Church. at 7:30 p.m. The next meeting is scheduled for December 22, at 7:00, at the United Presbyterian Church.

# # #

Please put names in alphabetic order.

THE STATUE OF LIBERTY

One of the first sights visitors see as they sail into the New York Harbor is the Statue of Liberty. She has stood as a symbol of freedom on Liberty Island since 1886.

The statue was given to the United States by the French people as a symbol of friendship. Bartholdi designed it. Edouard de Laboulaye, a French historian who admired American political institutions, made the suggestion that France present the statue to the United States. The statue arrived from France dismantled in June of 1885. When it was completed in October of 1886, President Cleveland held a dedication ceremony.

The statue is a woman draped with classical robes, who wears a crown with seven spokes. At her feet lie broken shackles left over from slavery life. Her extended right arm holds a torch. In her left hand, she carries a law book inscribed with the date of July 4, 1776. The statue weighs 225 tons, and there are 167 steps from the land level to the top of the pedestal. Visitors can ride the elevator to the top of the pedestal, and from there, they can climb a spiral staircase into the statue's crown.

A two-and-a-half million dollar building was opened in 1972 at the base of the statue by President Nixon. Visitors are able to view photographs, artifacts, and posters. After two years of extensive renovation, the statue was reopened in July of 1986. During this renovation time, new elevators were installed, the framework of the statue was repaired, and its surface was cleaned.

400

Conservatory Opera Company
~~500~~ Lewis Drive
Columbia, MO 65211-7762

For Release: Upon Receipt

Contact: Eric Brown, (314) 555-9984

Columbia, MO, October ~~22~~ *21*, 19--. The Conservatory Opera Company has installed Lynn Marcum as president for 19--, named ~~Anne~~ *Anna* Baker president-elect, and *will* heard a preview of its November production of Giacomo Puccini's "La Boheme" *on November 3.*

On behalf of the board, Ms. Marcum announced the establishment of the Sally Atwood Endowment Fund for Principal Artists. Honoring last year's outgoing president of the company, the Fund is designed to bring "the very best singers to Columbia," Marcum said.

Reports on the past year, hailed as a highly successful one by Marcum, showed that more than 2,400 people heard the Karen Copeland recital last spring; and over 2,700--almost a capacity crowd in the Grant Memorial Auditorium--attended the November presentation of Wolfgang Amadeus Mozart's "Don Giovanni."

The company staged its first production--"La Traviata"--in 1981. Productions have been staged each fall since, for a single performance, under the baton of Harry Jackson, artistic director.

Marcum said the company plans ~~two~~ *three* presentations of its main opera of the season beginning in 1990. She said the audience for opera in Columbia is increasing, and the company believes ~~two~~ *three* productions, with a potential audience of nearly ~~6,000~~ *7,800*, are feasible.

Because of the success of last year, this year's opera budget will increase to approximately $250,000.

THE STATUE OF LIBERTY

One of the first sights visitors see as they sail into the New
York Harbor, is the Statue of Liberty. She has stood as a symbol of
freedom on Liberty Island since 1886.

The statue was given to the United States by the French people
as a symbol of friendship. Bartholdi designed it. Edouard de
Laboulaye, a French historian who admired American political institutions, made the suggestion that France present the statue to
the United States. The statue arrived from France dismantled in
June of 1885. When it was completed in October of 1886, President
Cleveland held a dedication ceremony.

The statue is a woman draped with classical robes, who wears a
crown with seven spokes. At her feet lie broken shackles left over
from slavery life. Her extended right arm holds a torch. In her
left hand, she carries a law book inscribed with the date of July 4,
1776. The statue weighs 225 tons, and there are 167 steps from the
land level to the top of the pedestal. Visitors can ride the
elevator to the top of the pedestal, and from there, they can climb
a spiral staircase into the statue's crown.

A two-and-a-half million-dollar building was opened in 1972 at
the base of the statue by President Nixon. Visitors are able to
view photographs, artifacts, and posters. After two years of extensive renovation, the statue was reopened in July of 1986. During
this renovation time, new elevators were installed, the framework of
the statue was repaired, and its surface was cleaned.

beginning in 1990   ②

(¶) Marcum said the company plans two presentations of its main opera of the season. She said the audience for opera in columbia is increasing, and the company believes two productions, with a potential audience of nearly 6,000, are too feasible. The company must plan two years in advance because of the need to sign get artists well a head of their actual appearance here.

(¶) This year's opera budget will increase to approximately $250,000. Also, an extensive opera education program is under way in the near by communities.

(¶) Guest artist Elana McCarley, who sang excerpts from "La Boheme" Monday Tuesday evening, is touring city and also county schools with the program. The city school program this year features visits by docents from the company. Mark Carpenter, head of the education committee program, said the culmination of the education program this year will be a March presentation of "Cinderella" and "Don Pasquale" for fifth, sixth, seventh and eighth graders.

(¶) New board members are Jane Curtis, Ann York, Philip Jenkins, Ruth Beaman, Philip Zinsser, Albert Chung, and Carmen Torres.

(¶) The annual meeting was held Tuesday, October 15, at the United Presbyterian Church.

# # #

The education program is supported by a grant from the Crawford Foundation.

PERSONAL COMPUTERS

(¶) The term personal computer is used to refer to the small, desktop, or even handheld computers. Due to the fact that their electronic circuitry is on a small silicon chip called a microprocessor, personal computers are smaller in size than many business computers and are also less expensive.

(¶) The first uses of personal computers were by hobbyists for laboratories and recreation. The leading uses of personal computers are for video games, business or office, homework, and as a learning tool for both children and adults.

(¶) Many transaction services are available for such activities as shopping, stock trading, sports, education, science, and medicine. There is an original fee paid by the user plus an hourly charge which varies depending on the time of day it is used and the modem running speed.

(¶) Personal computers can be instructed to perform a wide variety of individual functions. The most popular are database, spreadsheet, and word processing. Database programs make it possible for users to store large amounts of information systematically. Spreadsheet programs are used to easily prepare tables for which predictions can be made, and "what if" questions can be answered. Word processing programs allow users to manipulate text and to make changes in copy before the final copy is printed. Also, personal computers are connected to other computers, and people are able to access databanks and to exchange data with other computers.

Conservatory Opera Company
500 Lewis Drive
Columbia, MO 6521-7762

For Release: Upon Receipt

Contact: Eric Brown, (314) 555-9984

(¶) Columbia, MO, October 22, 19--. The Conservatory Opera Company has installed Lynn Marcum as president for 19--, named Anne Baker president-elect, and heard a preview of its November production of Giacomo Puccini's "La Boheme."

(¶) On behalf of the board, Ms. Marcum announced the establishment of the Sally Atwood Endowment Fund for Principal Artists. Honoring last year's outgoing president of the company, the Fund is designed to bring "the very best singers to Columbia," Marcum said.

(¶) Reports on the past year, hailed as a highly successful one by Marcum, showed that more than 2,400 people heard the Karen Copeland recital last spring; and over 2,700 -- almost a capacity crowd in the Grant Memorial Auditorium -- attended the November presentation of Wolfgang Amadeus Mozart's "Don Giovanni."

(¶) The company staged its first production -- "La Traviata" -- in 1981. Productions have been staged each fall since, for a single performance, under the baton of Harry Jackson, artistic director.

ELECTRONIC MUSIC

Electronic music is a form of music composition in which sounds are produced electronically. Electronic devices are used to produce and manipulate sound design during its composition and performance that have a specific tone, range, pitch, and loudness. These sounds may be recorded on magnetic tape to create a composition, and they are played back through loudspeakers.

How are electronic sounds created? They may be created through electrical means, such as electronic sound synthesizers that originate and control sound. The composer directs the process of synthesizing, recording, and transforming the sounds into a musical composition. Electronic signals can be synthesized by the use of digital and analog computers. Electronic music composers can combine, modify, and distort the sounds with recorded sounds, such as wind, rain, and car noises.

In the early 1900s, equipment that could produce electronic music appeared in the U.S., France, and Russia. It was not until the late 1940s that this form of music became popular. ¶ With electronic music, the technical possibilities and expression range open to composers have increased. This music has become a part of all aspects of music. The increasing popularity of electronic music will expand as the cost of synthesizers decreases.

Job 5 Compose several short paragraphs on one of the following topics: 1) My Three Main Hobbies; 2) My Leisure Time Activities; or 3) Personal Traits Admired in Other People. Give your composition a proper heading; revise and rekey it in correct format. Correct errors.

2

The big advantage to selecting a 15-year term is the savings in total interest. For the same $50,000 mortgage we discussed earlier, the 30-year mortgage interest cost is $91,606.00, compared to $39,949.60 for the 15-year term. The savings for choosing the 15-year mortgage is $51,656.40 or 56 percent. Over half of the interest can be saved by choosing a 15-year term with payments of only 27 percent higher.

Admittedly, the 15-year mortgage loan is not for everyone. Because your payments will be larger, you may need a larger income to qualify, or you may need a larger down payment. As with all financial services, you should make sure these terms fit your financial situation. A Reynolds Credit Union loan officer is willing to sit down with you and help make sure a 15-year mortgage will work for you and your family. If you have questions, please do not hesitate to contact your nearest branch office.

# # #

The quality of a book review will be judged by how carefully the reader has read the book, how well the content has been understood, and how clearly reactions have been presented.

To write a review, answer the following questions: What was the purpose of the book? What methods were used to accomplish the purpose? Was the purpose worth accomplishing?

Include in the introduction the name, author, date of publication, type of work, and principal characters. Based on the questions you asked yourself earlier, develop a short summary which interprets the meaning of the book. If possible, use quotations to support your ideas. Conclude your report by analyzing the quality and the theme of the book. If using a word processor, use appropriate editing functions (see page 47). Refer to proofreader's marks, page 46, as needed. Proofread and correct all errors before removing or printing a final copy.

Layout Guides

The following book reviews are to be keyed from the model, rough draft, script, and corrected script. The following guidelines are but one acceptable form for formatting book reviews:

1. Margins: Top margin, first page, is 9 blank lines for pica and 11 blank lines for elite type. Side margins are 1", and the bottom margin is at least 1" inch (6 blank lines).
2. DS (double-space) the text and indent the first line of paragraphs 5 spaces.
3. Center the title in ALL CAPS.
4. QS (quadruple-space) below the title to first paragraph.
5. For second and subsequent pages, key the page number on line 6 at the right margin and continue keying the book review on line 8.

SILAS MARNER line 10, pica
by DS DS
George Eliot
QS

1"

Silas Marner was written in 1861 and is considered by noted critics as Eliot's best novel. The plot is domestic realism--it is simple in nature; the action is limited; and the strength of the novel lies in its description of the characters.

Silas Marner, the weaver of Raveloe, is an honest, sincere man. His life has been disrupted by a false accusation of a theft. For years, he lives a desolate existence with the sole companionship of his loom. While away from his cottage, he is robbed of his gold. He is saved from despair by finding a little yellow-haired girl whom he names Eppie. Silas lavishes the whole passion of his frustrated nature upon her. Her affection and devotion to Silas make him a sympathetic man again. He returns to a more wholesome and normal life. Eppie and Aaron, a village boy whom she has known for years, grow up together. The story becomes more complicated with the lives of Dunstan and Godfrey Cass and with identification of Eppie's real father. After 16 years, Silas returns to Lantern Yard where the real thief is discovered; Silas's good name is restored. This novel ends with the marriage of Eppie and Aaron. Silas has reaped his rewards; he is a grateful, happy man.

Silas depicts patience, suffering, and virtue. Eliot says that the book "is intended to set in a strong light the remedial influences of pure, natural, human relations."

(at least 1")

SILAS MARNER line 12, elite
by DS DS
George Eliot
QS

1"

Silas Marner was written in 1861 and is considered by noted critics as Eliot's best novel. The plot is domestic realism--it is simple in nature; the action is limited; and the strength of the novel lies in its description of the characters.

Silas Marner, the weaver of Raveloe, is an honest, sincere man. His life has been disrupted by a false accusation of a theft. For years, he lives a desolate existence with the sole companionship of his loom. While away from his cottage, he is robbed of his gold. He is saved from despair by finding a little yellow-haired girl whom he names Eppie. Silas lavishes the whole passion of his frustrated nature upon her. Her affection and devotion to Silas make him a sympathetic man again. He returns to a more wholesome and normal life. Eppie and Aaron, a village boy whom she has known for years, grow up together. The story becomes more complicated with the lives of Dunstan and Godfrey Cass and with identification of Eppie's real father. After 16 years, Silas returns to Lantern Yard where the real thief is discovered; Silas's good name is restored. This novel ends with the marriage of Eppie and Aaron. Silas has reaped his rewards; he is a grateful, happy man.

Silas depicts patience, suffering, and virtue. Eliot says that the book "is intended to set in a strong light the remedial influences of pure, natural, human relations."

(at least 1")

Reynolds Credit Union
1900 Bellefield Avenue
Pittsburgh, PA 15250-3390

Pittsburgh, PA, July 7, 19--.

For release: Immediately

Contact: Marie Cortez, (412)555-9000

The Reynolds Credit Union has unveiled a new *5-year* Adjustable Rate Mortgage *(ARM)* loan with a maximum term of ~~fifteen~~ *15* years. If you are in the market for a new home or would like to re finance your existing mortgage, you should look into this type of loan.

The major benefit of the 15-year term is the tremendous savings realized on interest payments. *In addition,* This loan is particularly advantageous if you would like to pay off your mortgage before the kids go to college or before any other major *financial* undertaking begins.

The interest rate for the 5-year ARM is currently 8.25 *percent*. This rate will remain constant for at least 5 years. At the end of 5 years *(and again at 10 years)*, the rate will change. The maximum change would be 2.5 percent at each 5-year period for a maximum increase of 5 percent over the life of the loan. The interest rate is tied to the one-year U.S. Treasury Bill rate; you may be assured of a third party index for objectivity *and a correct reflection of market conditions.*

You might expect that cutting the term of your mortgage in half might double your monthly payment. Instead, a marginal increase in payments ~~are~~ *is* actually realized. For instance, compare the $393.35 payment of a $50,000 loan for 30 years at 8.*2*5 percent to the $4*99*.72 payment for the same amount and rate for 15 years. The difference in the payments is $106.37. Just think, for 27 percent more in payments, your home may be paid off in half the *customary* time.

THE SCARLET LETTER

by

Nathaniel Hawthorne

<u>The Scarlet Letter</u>, published in 1850, is considered to be Hawthorne's best writing and one of the ten greatest American novels. The main theme of the novel is sin and the effect sin has on both the individual and on society.

The story covers events in Boston between 1642 and 1650. Hester Prynne was found guilty of adultery, and many people disagreed with the light sentence that she received. Women convicted of this crime were usually put to death, but Hester's sentence was to stand for three hours on a pillory platform and to wear a scarlet "A" embroidered on the bodice of her dress for the rest of her life.

Hester settled in a small cottage on the edge of town where she worked as a seamstress to support herself and her daughter, Pearl. The Reverend Dimmesdale used his influence to persuade the governor that Hester should be allowed to keep Pearl. Hester's estranged husband, Dr. Roger Chillingsworth, was able to figure out that Reverend Dimmesdale was Pearl's father.

Hester persuaded Dimmesdale to leave the country and promised to go with him. Before they were to leave for England, Dimmesdale stood on the scaffold in front of a large crowd and tore his ministerial garments, confessed his guilt, and died in Hester's arms. Hester and Pearl lived in England until Pearl got married, and then Hester returned to her cottage near Boston.

Blackstone Hotel
4300 Circle Drive
Cincinnati, OH 45241-2290

For Release: Upon Receipt

Contact: Susan Yen, (513) 555-3310

Cincinnati, OH, October 5, 19--. The sales and marketing executives of Blackstone Hotel will hold an early bird breakfast meeting Friday, October 25, at 7:15 a.m., in Conference Room D at the Blackstone Hotel. John M. Stork, CPA, will present a program on "How the New Tax Law Affects You." This program is open to the general public for a $7.95 breakfast fee.

According to Stork, the changes brought about by the Tax Reform Act of 1986 are the most sweeping in the nation's history, and virtually every individual and corporate taxpayer will feel its effect. Most of the provisions are very complex and will be phased in gradually over the next several years.

Treasurer since 1982 of the Blackstone Hotel, Stork is a member of the American Institute of CPAs and the Association of Public Speakers. He is active in various community activities and acts as treasurer for Cincinnati Mental Health Association. A native of Columbus, Ohio, Stork received a B.S. in Mathematics from Truman College and has completed graduate work at Atkins University.

The early bird breakfasts will be held the third Friday of every month at the Blackstone Hotel. The topic of next month's program will be announced later this month.

# # #

THE SCARLET LETTER

by

Nathaniel Hawthorne

The Scarlet Letter, published in 1850, is considered to be ~~Hawthorne's best writing and~~ one of the ten greatest American novels. The main theme of ~~the~~ _this_ novel is sin and the effect _of_ sin ~~has~~ on both the individual and on society.

The story ~~covers events~~ _occurs_ in Boston, _Massachusetts,_ between 1642 and 1650. Hester Prynne was found guilty of adultery, and many people disagreed with the ~~light~~ sentence ~~that~~ she received. ~~Women convicted of this crime were usually put to death, but,~~ Hester's sentence was to stand for three hours on a pillory platform and to wear a scarlet "A" embroidered on the bodice of her dress for the rest of her life.

Instead of leaving Boston, Hester settled in a small cottage on the edge of town where she _was able to_ work~~ed~~ as a seamstress to support herself and her daughter, Pearl. The Reverend Dimmesdale, _whose church she had disgraced,_ used his influence to persuade the governor ~~that~~ _to permit_ Hester ~~should be allowed~~ to keep Pearl. Hester's estranged husband, Dr. Roger Chillingsworth, was able to figure out that Reverend Dimmesdale was Pearl's father.

Hester persuaded _Reverend_ Dimmesdale to leave the country and promised to go with him. Before ~~they were to~~ leav_ing_ for England, _Reverend_ Dimmesdale stood on the scaffold in front of a large crowd and ~~tore his ministerial garments,~~ confessed his guilt; _then he_ and died in Hester's arms. Hester and Pearl lived in England until Pearl got married, and then Hester returned to her cottage near Boston.

News releases announce items of special interest to the news media. They are often composed and formatted in the office and then transmitted to the local newspaper for editing and publishing. News releases are written using the direct approach—main facts are mentioned in the initial paragraphs and lesser facts are presented later. Positioning facts in a news release is one of the best ways to achieve emphasis and to increase readability and interest.

News releases are often prepared on preprinted forms designed by a particular company. They may, however, be prepared on plain paper with the proper heading information added. See model below.

Layout Guide

1. Side and bottom magins: 1" side margins; at least 1" bottom margin.
2. Key the company name and address SS at the left margin, beginning on line 10, pica or line 12, elite.
3. DS after address information and key the heading "For Release:" ; the time of release information is placed 2 spaces after heading.
4. DS after time of release information and key the heading "Contact:"; begin keying the name and phone number of the contact person 2 spaces after the heading.
5. QS to body of news release (which always begins with the city, state, and date). Paragraphs are double-spaced with the first line indented 5 spaces.
6. For second and subsequent pages, key the page number on line 6 at the right margin and continue keying the news release on line 8.
7. A double space below the last line of the release, center the symbols ### to indicate the end of the release.

---

line 12, elite
Evens University line 10, pica
840 Arlee Drive
Greensboro, NC 27401-3215 DS
For Release: Immediately DS
Contact: Mary Anne Whitney, (919) 555-7721 QS

Greensboro, NC, June 11, 19--. The Class of 19-- will carry a heavy responsibility for shaping a new age in human history during the next 50 years, as more than 2,500 graduates were told at the Evens University at the 90th annual commencement exercise on Sunday.

Dr. Paula Schmitz, an accomplished attorney, educator, author, and one of the first women to be ordained as a priest of the Episcopal Church, told the students that humanity stands at the close of an era that began with the Renaissance. She said the new age presents a challenge for today's students to withstand the "torrents of change" and to devise "your own solutions to the problems of your era."

Dr. Schmitz suggested several "resources and values" that need to be continually cultivated: resilience of spirit, capacity for continuing growth, commitment to social and ethical goals beyond personal ambitions, and the capacity for hope that extends beyond the life spans of today's young adults. Dr. Schmitz pointed to altruistic leaders, such as Golda Meir and Eleanor Roosevelt, as role models for today's emerging adults. She praised these leaders for having the insight to pursue goals and dreams that would not be attained in their lifetimes.

(at least 1")

---

2 line 6

Chancellor Stan Morgan called on the graduates to set high line 8 expectations for themselves. "The level of experience that we adopt for ourselves," Chancellor Morgan declared, "does have a significant effect on our ultimate achievements as persons and as a people." He said that education has "equipped you for enlightened leadership" and admonished the graduates not to "allow timid vision and meager goals to hamper the use of your abilities."

More than 18,000 persons attended the commencement ceremonies. Among the dignitaries present were Tony Sadowski, chair of the Evans University Board of Trustees, and Greensboro's Mayor Lance McClures, who is also serving on the University's Board of Trustees.

Lara M. Ramey of Greensboro, an insurance and broadcasting executive, was awarded an honorary Doctor of Science degree. In addition, a new Evens University building is to be named for her. Dr. Ramey and her husband Kurt established the Creative Artist's Scholarship Fund and have supported many other university programs.

Two retired faculty members also received honorary degrees. A Doctor of Fine Arts was awarded to Danielle Hayes of Greensboro. Ms. Hayes is an internationally acclaimed concert pianist and was the Evens University artist-in-residence from 1963 to 1975. Carlos Mendez of Greensboro was awarded the degree of Doctor of Literature. DS

ROBINSON   CRUSOE
by
Daniel   Defoe

This adventure romance novel was first published in 1719 and is as widely read today as it was when it was first published.

His father wanted him to study law, but Robinson Crusoe chose to go to sea. Almost immediately, a storm caused him to become ill. He vowed that if God spared him he would go home; but when conditions improved, he forgot his vow and pursued other adventures.

After being captured, he was sold into slavery. He escaped and became a sugar planter in South America. In an attempt to sail to Africa, his ship was wrecked; and he was the only survivor. He carried necessities from the ship wreckage to a place where he could build a shelter. He spent twelve years planting barley and corn and raising goats for food.

One Friday morning, he was able to rescue a man from a group of savages. This man, whom he named Friday, became his trusted companion for the rest of his stay on the island. He taught Friday everything he knew, including how to speak English. Crusoe also helped Friday rescue his father from a group of savages who were holding him prisoner. Friday and his father settled on the island. Crusoe returned to England after twenty-eight years. Except for one trip to the old island, he did not travel any more but planned to end his days in peace.

③

Vice President

(TT) Don Rodriguez reported the ~~belief~~ *recommendation* of the Ad Hoc Committee on fraternities and sororities. It was reported that these groups be recognized for a trial period of ~~one~~ *two* years. A second committee is being appointed to ~~setup proper procedures,~~ develop operational guidelines.

(TT) Questions posed by assembly members included concerns about hazing policies, *possible discrimination,* blackballing, and secret meetings. It was moved that the assembly await its recommendation until members have had an opportunity to study the report of the ~~first~~ second committee. The motion carried.

Adjournment

(TT) A motion for adjournment was made *seconded,* and passed. The meeting adjourned at 5:15 p.m.

QS

[Wanda Thies, Recording Secretary

THE TRAGEDY OF MACBETH
by
William Shakespeare

center; DS

QS

Shakespeare's romantic tragedy of retribution and ambition, *The Tragedy of Macbeth*, was written about 1610. The prose story was recorded in Holinshed's *Chronicles*. Every scene is painted with horror. ¶ Having returned from a campaign, Macbeth and Banquo meet three witches who prophesy that Macbeth will become King of Scotland and that Banquo's sons will reign in Scotland. Lady Macbeth hears of the prophesy and convinces Macbeth to murder the King. Macbeth is crowned at Scone. Since he fears Banquo, Macbeth has his friend murdered. Macbeth, already deeply in crime, has no recourse but to become a bloody tyrant. He ends his career at Dunsinane Castle, where the slain King's sons, Malcolm and Macduff, and the English soldiers and Scottish rebels meet. The witches have told Macbeth that he shall not perish unless Birnam wood comes to Dunsinane and that no one of woman born shall have mortal power over him. As they approach the castle, the enemy cuts branches of Birnam wood. Macbeth is terrified but relying on the other prophesy of the witches, he goes to battle. The prophesy is fulfilled, and Macbeth is overcome and beheaded by Macduff. ¶ Macbeth is an imaginative and ambitious man whose wife drives him to murder. He meets Macduff, who tells him that he isn't strictly of woman born.

②

(TT) Recent federal legislation has prohibited a mandatory retirement age under 70. Institutions operating under tenure systems are exempt from such limitations until June 30, 19--, provided they declare themselves to be under that exemption. The Board of Governors has adopted such a statement and has asked that each campus make this a part of their tenure regulations.

(TT) Dr. Alice Tetreault noted that the Academic Cabinet adopted this resolution at their last meeting; she moved that the assembly also recommend that the Salem College tenure regulations be amended to reflect this change. The motion carried.

(TT) Dr. James Clotfelter reported that following a recommendation that Salem College revise its science certification programs, Dean Yen, Dean Reilly, and he met with the chairpersons of the biology, chemistry, and physics departments in order to study such programs on other campuses. A one-page summary of this proposal will be circulated to the entire faculty, and the full proposal will be given to the deans and department heads. Dr. Clotfelter moved that the proposal be tabled until the next meeting. The motion was seconded and passed.

An unbound report is one in which the pages will remain in loose-leaf form. The report will not be bound at the left or at the top; rather, it is usually stapled in the upper left corner. An unbound report is sometimes placed in a folder or company binder to secure and to protect it and to maintain confidentiality.

Form and arrangement of reports are often determined by a company, an office preference, or a school policy. Companies that require regular reports have found it convenient to use a standard format and binder.

Headings may be placed throughout a report for the reader's convenience. Textual citations are also often used instead of footnotes. When textual citations are used, a reference list is placed at the end of the report arranged in alphabetic order. See models below.

Layout Guides

1. Top margin: First page, line 10 for pica and line 12 for elite; succeeding pages, line 8 with the page number on line 6 at the right margin.
2. Side margins, 1"; bottom margin, at least 1".
3. DS the text and indent paragraphs 5 spaces.
4. Main heading: Center and key in ALL CAPS; if a two-line main heading, DS between heading lines; QS between heading and first paragraph.
5. Side heading: Key at left margin and underline; initial cap main words; DS above and DS below heading.
6. Paragraph heading: Indent to paragraph point and underline; follow heading with a period; initial cap *only* the first word of the heading.
7. Textual citation: Place in parentheses; include last name of author(s), year of publication, and indicate page number(s) if applicable.
8. Reference list: Center main heading "REFERENCES," and QS to first entry; key list in alphabetic order; SS references, but DS between them; begin first line of each entry at left margin; indent all other lines 5 spaces; place list a QS below last line of report or on a separate page.

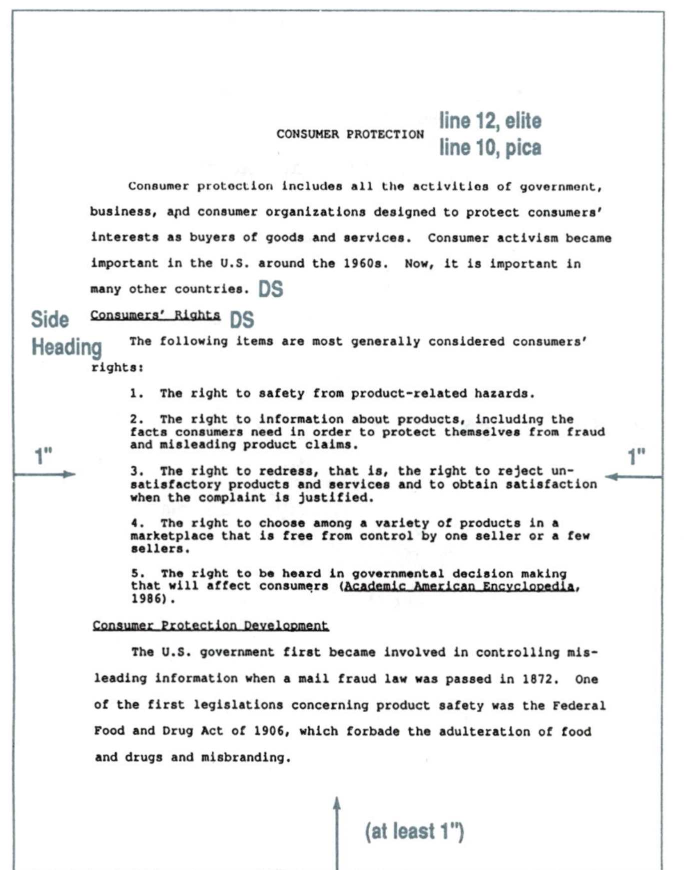

(Annette Johannesen,

Salem College

MINUTES OF FACULTY ASSEMBLY

<u>Time</u> *and Place*

monthly
The regular meeting of the Salem College Faculty Assembly was held in the Richmond Room of the Moravian House on Wednesday, November 27, 19--.

3
The meeting was called to order at 4:30 p.m. by President Peter Sanchez; Wanda Thies was the recording secretary. Other members <u>present included</u>: Rebecca Askew, Robert Bondurant, Jim Clotfelter, Betty Erlandson, Charles Kefter, Augustine Laurel, Kevin Lebensburger, Walter Liebscher, Allen Miller, Rosamond Putzel, Dana Ramsey, Don Rodriguez, Elise Stephens, and Alice Tetreault.

— (Starr Sordelett,

<u>Approval of Minutes</u>

O   *e*
The minutes of the October 15, 19--, meeting, which had been mailed to assembly members on November 5, were approved.

<u>Old Business</u>

by the Committee on Faculty Government
two
The ~~one~~ proposed amendment to the Instrument of Government made, which had been placed on the table at the October 15 meeting, ~~was~~ *were* brought before the assembly for ~~discussion.~~ *action.*

It was proposed and moved that the following changes be made in the salem College Instrument of Government:

(VII)   *IV*
1. Delete the last sentence of Article A, Section 5c *O*   *DS*
2. Delete Article A, Section 6b, and replace it with:

N   *assembly*
Election for all positions or offices requiring vote shall be held on a designated date at least three weeks before the last day of classes of the spring semester. *The motion carried.*

<u>New Business</u>

in Management Information Systems
Salem College Long-Range Plan contained approval for two new degrees programs on this campus, President Sanchez reported. These programs are (1) Master of Arts, and (2) Master of Arts in Accounting. Salem College will begin developing these programs in the individual departments for processing the Graduate Executive Council.

(Graduate Board and the

through

planning—

HOW THE PERSONAL COMPUTER WORKS

What makes a personal computer (PC) work? A PC has many working parts. However, let's consider the CPU, RAM, and DOS.

Microprocessor

The main brain of the computer is usually contained on one
solid-state "chip," called the microprocessor. Also known as the
CPU or Central Processing Unit, the microprocessor performs mathematical and logical operations, such as sorting, comparing, and
manipulating information. A computer doesn't think; it uses complex
sets of instructions (programs) to perform everyday business tasks.
Your program loads into the computer's memory, where the microprocessor then pulls out specific chunks of instructions in response
to your typed commands.

Random Access Memory

Random Access Memory (RAM), which is located on a bank of chips
inside the computer, stores a program's instructions and your data,
while the microprocessor performs the tasks the program demands.
The information you place into the program stays in memory until you
store your work in a file. File storage is normally accomplished
with a magnetic disk. A computer can have both a floppy-disk drive
and a hard-disk drive.

Stored information and RAM memory are measured in units that
are called bytes (O'Brien, 1988, 155). A byte is a basic grouping
of bits (smallest element of data) that the computer operates on as

MINUTES OF THE FBLA CHAPTER MEETING

QS

<u>Time and Place</u>

The regular meeting of the FBLA Chapter was held at 1:30 p.m., September 11, 19--, in the school's cafeteria. In the absence of the president, the vice president presided.

<u>Approval of Minutes</u>

After roll call, the minutes of the previous meeting were read and approved.

<u>Treasurer's Report</u>

The treasurer reported the receipts of $45.00 in dues, no disbursements, and a balance of $109.14.

<u>Committee Reports</u>

The committee on chapter activities reported the types of activities to be planned during the next nine months. It was moved by Freddie Eisenberg that a committee be appointed to plan a social for the December meeting. Seconded by Tom Anderson, the motion carried. It was then moved by Louise Wright that the president act as the representative of the chapter at the upcoming national conference. It was seconded by Joyce Yang. The motion carried.

<u>New Business and Adjournment</u>

An invitation to the members to attend the FBLA regional meeting on November 19 was read. The meeting was adjourned at 2:30 p.m. QS

David Gerringer, Secretary

a single unit. The capacity of a computer's primary and ~~its~~

secondary storage devices are usually ~~expressed~~ *defined* in terms of bytes,

such as kilobytes for thousands and megabytes for millions of

bytes. ~~The~~ *a* byte becomes the basic unit of data in most modern

computer systems.

Operating System

~~Every~~ *a* computer uses an operating system to organize certain

internal functions. The operating system acts as an internal

manager in your system. On some systems, especially home and

personal computers, the operating system, or portions thereof, is

recorded permanently into the internal memory circuits of the com-

puter (Adams and Wagner, 1986, 192). The Disk Operating System or

DOS organizes the internal workings of the personal computer and is

formally referred to as MS/DOS, ~~(after the system's developer, Micro-~~

~~Soft).~~ DOS translates *the* commands *you* type at the keyboard into instruc-

tions *that* the CPU understands.

References

Adams, David R., and Gerald E. Wagner. <u>Computer Information Sys-

tems: An Introduction</u>. Cincinnati: South-Western Publishing Co.,

1986.

O'Brien, James A. <u>Information Systems in Business Management</u>.

Homewood, IL: Richard D. Irwin, Inc., 1988.

MINUTES OF MEETING OF NATIONAL HONOR SOCIETY

<u>Time and Place</u>

The regular monthly meeting of the National Honor Society was held in the library on Wednesday, February 11, 19--. The meeting was called to order at 1:15 p.m. by President Alexia Snowberg; Fred Seng was the recording secretary. Other members present included: Ruthie Abbott, Beatrice Erlandson, Donald Gerringer, Louise Hinz, Ted Iscaro, Betty Lautermilch, Frances Long, Anna Moulton, Walter Pritchard, Jennifer Riches, Toshi Rodriguez, and Susan Watanabe.

<u>Approval of Minutes</u>

The minutes of the January 5 meeting were read and approved.

<u>New Business</u>

It was proposed and moved to delete the last three sentences of Article IX, Section 4a. The motion carried.

Mrs. Anna Moulton gave a brief history of the National Honor Society.

Questions posed by various members included concerns about initiation procedures, next year's national dues, refreshments at the next regular meeting, and inactive members.

<u>Adjournment</u>

There being no further business, a motion for adjournment was made, seconded, and passed. The meeting adjourned at 2:00 p.m.

Fred Seng, Secretary

TYPES OF CREDIT CARDS

Credit cards allow people to charge goods and services at business places that accept these cards. Many types of banks, oil companies, and business firms issue credit cards. To obtain one, you must have a record of paying your bills promptly. Each card has the cardholder's name and card number. When a purchase is made, the card must be presented (_The World Book Encyclopedia_, 1987).

Bank Credit Cards

Bank credit cards have become very popular. MasterCard and VISA are two of the most popular. Most of the banks in the U.S. are part of the worldwide bank charge-card system. There usually is an annual fee that must be paid for the privilege of using the card.

Bank credit cards are issued to people whose credit ratings meet banks' standards. A bank credit card indicates that the credit rating of the cardholder is good. Agreements are made between banks and various merchants to accept the charge cards. Customers like bank credit cards because they are accepted by so many businesses throughout the U.S. and in several foreign countries (Daughtrey, Ristau, and Eggland, 1986, 374).

Travel and Entertainment Credit Cards

These cards are similar to bank charge cards. However, an independent firm performs the functions for T & E accounts that a bank performs with bank

Special reports are often required to be formatted and keyed in the business office. These reports may follow different styles. However, they should be organized in order to achieve unity and completeness. In this section, you will key minutes.

Minutes of meetings are the written records of business meetings—informal or formal. Minutes should contain an accurate account of the meeting by reporting on the topics discussed, votes taken, and decisions reached. Also, minutes should include the kind of meeting (regular or special), location, and date of the meeting. The form in which the minutes are to be keyed is usually determined by the company. They should be written in the third person and with no personal comments. Word-for-word reporting is usually not necessary, except in the case of resolutions and amendments. Minutes are often duplicated and distributed to the membership. Minutes may be keyed in either leftbound or unbound format. In this section, you will key minutes in unbound format. See model below.

Layout Guides

1. Side and bottom magins: 1" side margins; at least 1" bottom margin.

2. Main heading: Center main heading in ALL CAPS on line 10, pica; line 12, elite. If two lines are needed, DS below first heading line to key the second line. QS to the body of the minutes.

3. If minutes are more than one page, SS the body, block paragraphs at left margin, and DS above and below paragraphs. If minutes are less than one page, DS the body and indent paragraphs 5 spaces (see model on page 80).

4. For second and following pages, key the page number on line 6 at the right margin and continue keying the minutes on line 8.

5. Enumerated items: SS each item but DS above and below each item. Block enumerated items at left margin.

6. DS above and below side headings.

7. When closing, QS after the body of the minutes and key a signature line from center point to the right margin. Then SS and key name and title of writer at center point.

Model — page 1:

line 12, elite
line 10, pica

MINUTES OF MEETING OF

STATE EMPLOYEES' CREDIT UNION ADVISORY BOARD

QS

Time and Place DS

The regular monthly meeting of the State Employees' Credit Union Advisory Board was held in the Conference Room of Alba Associates, Austin, Texas, December 6, 19--. DS

The meeting was called to order at 7:30 p.m. by Dwight Story, presiding officer; Beatrice Garcia was the recording secretary. Other members present included: Lucille Benfield, Theodore Daughtery, Michael Edelston, Patty Emmett, Betty Fulton, Everett Greene, Samuel Hutchison, Mildred Johnson, Henry Litchford, Carl Love, Antonio Markez, Elizabeth McNeill, Gloria Pons, Gwendolyn Starling, Bernice Willers, and Robert Zimmerman. DS

Approval of Minutes

The minutes of the August 15, 19--, meeting were read and approved as distributed.

Committee Reports

1"   Mr. Story called on Henry Litchford for the report of the branch manager. Ms. Garcia distributed a chart comparing monthly totals of new members, gross amount of loans, number of loans, share deposits, share withdrawals, and demand deposits for the months of July, August, September, October, and November for 19--. The chart clearly depicted substantial increases in these areas for these months. There was particular interest in the large increase in demand deposits. DS   1"

President Story asked the board if the Credit Union was still considering free checking as had been discussed previously. After a discussion, it was decided that due to the minimal cost factor and the fact that most banks offer free checking, the Credit Union would institute free checking at this time. It was mentioned that members who open checking accounts with the Credit Union were satisfied with the $200.00 minimum balance policy. DS

Ms. Garcia was called upon to report on the status of the Credit Union with regards to loans, share deposits, and demand deposits. Charts were distributed by Ms. Garcia. The charts illustrated the yearly totals for new members, number of loans, gross loans, share deposits, share withdrawals, and demand deposits for the last two years.

(at least 1")

Model — page 2:

2 line 6
line 8

Mr. Everett Greene was called upon by President Story for the district report. Mr. Greene gave a summary of action taken by the board of directors: DS

1. A 9 percent interest dividend will be paid through March 31, 19--. DS

2. The money order fee is increased from $1.50 to $2.50, effective January 1, 19--.

3. The rate charged on term notes is increased.

4. The entry of the Credit Union into the secondary mortgage market is approved.

1"   President Story stated that the board of directors had decided to use the secondary mortgage market in order to provide a source of money to meet member demands for mortgage loans.   1"

Mrs. Pons reported that two new offices would be opening soon, one in Amarillo and in San Antonio.

Adjournment

President Story announced March 5 as the date of the next meeting. A motion for adjournment was made, seconded, and passed. The meeting was adjourned at 9:30 p.m. QS

Beatrice Garcia, Secretary

(center point)

charge-card accounts. The T&E cards, such as American[2] Express and Diners' Club, are used at a variety of hotels and motels, restaurants, stores, and other businesses. Purchases are billed like bank charge-card purchases, and T&E card users pay annual fees for the privilege of having the card.

Travelers especially like T&E credit cards because they do not have to carry much cash with them. Firms which accept T&E credit cards often find that their sales increase because more customers are attracted when T&E cards can be used.

<u>Oil Company Credit Cards</u>

Most consumers find it convenient to have credit cards with oil companies from whom they frequently purchase gasoline. The oil companies like to extend credit to encourage consumers to purchase their products.

Many oil companies issue their own credit cards. As with banks, these accounts are opened for customers who apply for credit and have their applications approved. Oil company credit cards can generally be used only for purchases from gasoline stations selling that company's brand of gasoline, for car maintenance, and for merchandise (Daughtrey et al., 1986, 377).

REFERENCES ← QS / ← QS

"Credit Card." <u>The World Book Encyclopedia</u>, 1987. DS

Daughtrey, Anne Scott, Robert A. Ristau, and Steven A. Eggland. <u>Introduction to Business: The Economy and You.</u> Cincinnati: South-Western Publishing Co., 1986.

(3)

1. There is an exponential relationship between the demands of managing the application portfolio and size of that portfolio. The huge application portfolios of the larger firms bring with them exponentially more managerial problems.

2. Medium-sized firms operate under severe personnel restrictions. A large firm has in place staff members whose sole job responsibility is to keep abreast of current technological advances. No medium-sized firm had such a mechanism in place.

<u>Conclusions</u>

Based upon this particular study, the following conclusions have emerged:

1. Within the area of computer technology, CEOs perceived a primary leadership challenge to exist in the arena of strategic management of information systems.

2. The perceived primary challenge in strategic management of information systems varies by firm size.

REFERENCES

Ashby, W. R. <u>Design for a Brain</u>. London: Chapman and Hall, 1960.

Bozeman, Barry, and Elliot Cole. "Scientific and Technical Information in Public Management." <u>Administration & Society</u> (February 1982), 479-493.

Emery, F. E., and E. L. Trist. "The Causal Texture of Organizational Environments." <u>Human Relations</u> (February 1965), 21-31.

Radford, K. J. <u>Information Systems for Strategic Decisions</u>. Reston: Reston Publishing Company, Inc., 1978.

HOW THE PERSONAL COMPUTER WORKS

What makes a personal computer (PC) work? A PC has many working parts. However, let's consider the CPU, RAM, and DOS.

Microprocessor *(Central Processing Unit*

The ~~main~~ brain of the computer is ~~usually~~ contained on ~~one~~ *a* solid-state "chip" called the microprocessor. Also known as the CPU or Central Processing Unit, the microprocessor performs mathematical and logical operations, such as sorting, comparing, and manipulating information. A computer doesn't *have the ability to* think; it uses complex sets of instructions (programs) to perform everyday business tasks. Your program loads into the computer's memory, where the microprocessor then pulls out specific ~~chunks~~ *sets* of instructions in response to your typed commands.

Random Access Memory

Random Access Memory (RAM), which is located on a bank of chips inside the computer, stores *the* program's instructions and your data; while the microprocessor *processes* ~~performs~~ the tasks the program demands. The information you place into the program ~~stays~~ *remains* in memory until you ~~store~~ *save* your work in a file. File storage is normally accomplished with a magnetic disk. A computer can have ~~both~~ a floppy-disk drive and a hard-disk drive.

Stored information and RAM memory are measured in units that are called bytes (O'Brien, 1988, 155). A byte is a basic grouping of bits (smallest element of data) that the computer operates on as

A hard-disk drive contains one or more enclosed hard metal disks which hold as much as fifty or more times the information than can a floppy disk, and a hard-disk drive can access information much more rapidly.

(2)

(¶) The research reported resulted from interviews with CEOs of selected firms. The purpose of this research was to determine CEOs' perceptions of leadership challenges they face in an era of technological turbulence. It was also of particular interest in noting challenges identified by CEOs of medium-sized firms that were not identified by CEOs of large firms.

(¶) Medium-sized firms were primarily concerned with the difficulties faced in (1) keeping abreast of current technological advances, (2) maintaining awareness of competitors' adaptations of computer technology, (3) selecting advances in computer technology for implementation, and (4) adapting selected technology to the specific needs of the firm. As a composite, these activities form the structural foundation of gatekeeping -- flow of information from the external to the internal environment of the organization through a medium bestowed with internal esteem (Bozeman and Cole, 1982).

(¶) This emphasis on gatekeeping, rather than on portfolio management, by medium-sized firms can be attributed to two factors:

2

a single unit. ~~The capacity of~~ a computer's primary storage and secondary storage devices are often ~~usually~~ defined in terms of bytes, such as kilobytes for thousands and megabytes for millions ~~of bytes~~. The ~~A~~ byte is ~~becomes~~ the basic unit of data in most modern computer systems.

<u>Operating System</u>

A computer uses an operating system to organize certain internal functions. On some systems, especially home and personal computers, the operating system is recorded permanently into the internal memory circuits of the computer (Reiss and Dolan, 1989, 277 ~~Adams and Wagner, 1986, 192~~). ~~The operating system acts as an internal manager in your system.~~ The Disk Operating System or DOS organizes the internal workings of the personal computer and is formally referred to as MS/DOS. DOS translates the commands you type at the keyboard into instructions that the CPU understands. DOS assists the Basic Input/Output System in moving information in and out of the system.

REFERENCES
< QS

Delete

~~Adams, David R., and Gerald E. Wagner. <u>Computer Information Systems: An Introduction</u>. Cincinnati: South-Western Publishing Co., 1986.~~

O'Brien, James A. <u>Information Systems in Business Management</u>. Homewood, IL: Richard D. Irwin, Inc., 1988.

Reiss, Levi, and Edwin G. Dolan. <u>Using Computers: Managing Change</u>. Cincinnati: South-Western Publishing Co., 1989.

COMPUTER TECHNOLOGY CHALLENGES OF
CHIEF EXECUTIVE OFFICERS _DS_

_QS_

Gwendolyn W. Loy   _Key at centerpoint_   Anne C. Steele
Florida State University   Temple University
Tallahassee, Florida   Philadelphia, _Pennsylvania_
~~Pennsylvania~~

_QS_

Introduction

    The environmental schema _postulated_ ~~stated~~ by Emery _and Trist_ provides a frame work for the categorization of the environment in which non-growth industrial _corporations must operate. For such firms,_ ~~must exist,~~ Today's environment fluctuates between two classifications--"disturbed-reactive" and "turbulent." A "disturbed-reactive" environment is one in which environmental factors are changing at a rate _and severity level_ that necessitates organizational adaptation for even minimal survival. An environment in which factor change is _not only_ rapid and severe but also interactive is known as "turbulent" (Ashby, 1960; Emery and Trist, 1965; Radford, 1978). From all indications, this will continue to be a contributing _ory_ factor into the next _decade_ ~~century~~. Dynamic and radical change in computer technology is one of the primary factors contributing to these environmental disturbances.

    Environment_al_ turbulence has _heightened_ ~~influenced~~ the Chief Executive Officers' (CEOs) awareness of the role that computer_s_ _technology_ plays in the profitability of a firm. _In response to this awareness, CEOs have recognized a new dimension in their leadership role that demands increased understanding of the technological revolution._

TYPES OF BUSINESS ~~ORGANIZATIONS~~ (Associations) — *make all caps*

All social ~~groups~~ *groupings* are organized for some ~~form~~ *type* of business *organization*. Business ~~enterprises~~ ~~customarily~~ *associations usually* take one of three ~~types~~ *forms*: ~~individual~~ proprietorships, partnerships, ~~or limited liability companies~~ or corporations.

~~Individual~~ Proprietorship

In a proprietorship, a single person holds the *entire* operation as *his or her* personal property, usually managing it on a day-to-day basis. ~~Most businesses are of this type.~~ Of the nearly 15,000,000 business establishments in the U. S. ~~in the late 20th century,~~ more than three-quarters *are* ~~wer individual~~ proprietorships. They tend to be small operatons, ~~most of them~~ with annual receipts of less than $50,000 (The New Encyclopaedia Britannica, 1987).

Partnership

The second form of *a* business ~~organization~~ *association* is a partnership. *A* ~~The~~ partnership is a business organization with two or more members, *Large membership is exemplified in* ~~as in the case of~~ large law and accounting firms, brokerage houses, and advertising agencies. This form of busines*s* is owned by the partners themselves; they may receive varying shares of the profits depending on their investment or contribution. Whenever a ~~member~~ *partner* leaves or a new ~~member~~ *partner* is added, the ~~firm~~ *business* must be reconstituted as a new partnership.

Special features. *Several* ~~The~~ distinguishing features of the partner- ship are the personal and unrestricted liability of each partner for *the debts and obligations of the firm and the right of each partner to participate in the management of the firm and to act as an agent of it in entering into legal transactions on its*

Guides for keying professional articles for publication vary with publishers. Before submitting an article, you should obtain the style for keying the article from the publisher. The guides listed here represent only one acceptable form of formatting articles. In this section you will be keying an unbound, 3-page article. If necessary, review basic formatting guidelines for an unbound report on page 11.

Layout Guides

Type the article as an unbound report taking note of the following:

1. Title: Center the title in ALL CAPS. If the title is long, use 2 lines and DS between lines. Then QS and block at left margin the following information, each on a separate single-spaced line: author's name, author's school or company, and the city and state of the author. (If there is more than one author, begin keying the second author's information at center point.) QS and begin keying the first paragraph.
2. On second and succeeding pages, key the title of the article on line 6 at the left margin. Key the page number on line 6 even with the right margin. DS and continue keying the article.
3. Textual citations: Place in parentheses at the appropriate point in the report. Include the last name of the author (unless it is mentioned in the text), the year of publication, and the page number(s) if applicable.
4. Reference list: Key references in alphabetic order using the following format:
   a. Center main heading "REFERENCES" a QS below the last line of the article.
   b. QS after the heading to the first entry.
   c. Begin the first line of each entry at the left margin; indent all other lines 5 spaces.
   d. SS each entry but DS between them.
5. Enumerated items: SS each item but DS above and below each item. Indent enumerated items 5 spaces from the left margin. Runover lines are blocked at the five-space indention point.

Example — page 1

ARTIFICIAL INTELLIGENCE AND EXPERT SYSTEMS *(line 12, elite / line 10, pica)*
QS

Doris Lucille Verrault
Colorado State University
Fort Collins, Colorado
QS

<u>Background</u> DS

    Artificial intelligence (AI) has been devoted primarily to research-oriented systems. AI software is likely to be discussed and evaluated as other software--how much it costs, how fast it runs, and how much memory and storage it requires. AI is becoming another form of data processing technology; data processing and AI will coexist (Schindler, 1986).

<u>AI Definitions</u>

    Winston defined AI as "the study of ideas which enables computers to do the things that make people seem intelligent" (1984, 1). Another way to characterize AI is in terms of the programming techniques and philosophies that have evolved from it. AI techniques permit programmers to present knowledge that is much more flexible and natural for humans to deal with than the algorithmic procedures used in traditional programming languages (Luconi, <u>et al.</u>, 1986).

<u>AI Applications</u>

    AI appears to have promising applications in (1) developing computer programs that can read, speak, or understand language as people use it in everyday conversation--commonly referred to as natural language processing; (2) developing smart robots to observe

(at least 1")

Example — page 2

ARTIFICIAL INTELLIGENCE AND EXPERT SYSTEMS   2 *(line 6 / line 8)*

the ongoing changes that take place as they move around in an environment; and (3) developing programs that use symbolic knowledge to simulate the behavior of human experts--commonly referred to as expert systems (Harmon and King, 1985, 1-49).

    Claims have been made to make systems think like a person rather than behave like a person. Expert Systems (ES) have come to the rescue of AI: A careful selection of a limited problem and a down-to-earth approach to its solution can result in an AI-based system that is highly useful in the business environment.

    Horwitt defines ES as programs that mimic the decision-making logic of human experts (1985). ES may be characterized as programs that function in a certain field of knowledge as a human expert would. The early knowledge-based systems were known as expert systems. Today, ES are often referred to as "knowledge systems."

QS

REFERENCES
QS

Harmon, Paul, and David King. <u>Expert Systems: Artificial Intelligence in Business</u>. New York: John Wiley and Sons, Inc., 1985.

Horwitt, Elisabeth. "Exploring Expert Systems." <u>Business Computer Systems</u> (March 1985), 49.

Luconi, Fred L., <u>et. al</u>. "Expert Systems: The Next Challenge for Managers." <u>Sloan Management Review</u> (Summer 1986), 3-14.

Schindler, Paul E. "AI is Becoming Just Another Form of DP." <u>Information Week</u> (May 5, 1986), 18.

Winston, P. H. <u>Artificial Intelligence</u>. Reading, MA: Addison-Wesley, 1984.

behalf. The civil-law systems of most continental European [2] countries have additionally always permitted a modified form of partnership, the limited partnership in which one or more of the partners are liable for the firm's debts only to the extent of the capital they contribute or agree to contribute. Such limited partners are prohibited from taking part in the management of the firm; however, if they do, they become personally liable without limit for the debts of the firm, together with the general partners (Brown and Clow, 1987, 141-142).

<u>Corporation</u>

The third form, the limited-liability company or corporation, denotes incorporated groups of persons--that is, a number of persons considered as a legal entity with property, powers, and liabilities separate from those of its members. This type of company is also legally separate from the individuals who work for the company, whether they are shareholders, employees, or both. The company can enter into legal relations with such individuals, make contracts with them, and sue and be sued by them. Most of the large industrial and commercial organizations are limited-liability companies or corporations.

The company or corporation, unlike a partnership, is formed not simply by an agreement entered into between its first members. It must also be registered at a public office or court designated by law, or otherwise obtain official acknowledgment of its existence. Under American law, the company or corporation is incorporated by filing the company's constitution signed by its

3

family. Those between 75 and 84 years old are looking for social contacts and organized activities. Congregate housing addresses this need. The last segment includes those over 85 years old who need help beyond meals and housekeeping. They need help in personal and health-care services.

Regional Migration

¶ Most elderly do not flee to the Sunbelt states. In fact, states with a high percentage of elderly are not unique to the Sunbelt. States that have recently suffered economic hardships, like many farm-belt states, have a high percentage of elderly. Even though the Sunbelt is not unique in its high elderly population, the highest projected increase in elderly population will be concentrated in the Sunbelt.[4]

¶ Elderly housing has been shown to represent a significant portion of total housing demand in the country, and this portion is expected to grow throughout the century. Communities need to provide housing to meet the specific needs of this large, diverse elderly group.

———————

[4] No doubt the projected growth rates reflect a continuation of young people migrating to other regions. The elderly population is expected to increase significantly, and rise as a share of total population, in every region through 1990.

This situation in the farm belt is caused by a large number of young individuals leaving these regions in search of employment opportunities elsewhere.

3

first members at the office of the state secretary.

Dividends. The shares of a company are freely transferable unless the company's constitution imposes restrictions on their transfer. Finally, a shareholder is only entitled to a dividend out of the company's profits when the dividend has been declared. Under American law, dividends are usually declared by the directors. If, however, shareholders believe that too small of a dividend has been paid in view of the company's profits, they may ask the court to direct payment of a reasonable dividend.

REFERENCES) center

Put references in alphabetic order.

"Business Organization." The New Encyclopaedia Brittannica, 1987.

Mietus, Norbert J., John E. Adamson, and Edward J. Conry. Applied Business Law. Cincinnati: South-Western Publishing Co., 1988.

Brown, Betty J., and John E. Clow. Our Business and Economic World. Boston: Houghton Mifflin Company, 1987.

Also, shares in a company do not expose the holder to unlimited liability.

(Mietus, Adamson, and Conry, 1988, 700)

2

Less than five percent of those 65 and over are con-
fined to their homes for health reasons.

The elderly population has been and will continue to
be one of the fastest growing segments of the population.
Since 1980, the growth rate for the elderly population has
slowed but still exceeds the overall rate of growth of
the country. It should continue to do so through 1990
and the remainder of the century.[3]

<u>Housing Needs</u>

Adequate housing is not a problem for the elderly.
Most elderly continue to live in the homes where they
reared their families long after they have retired. However,
their homes are often too big and expensive to maintain. Therefore, future housing must offer housing that
is congenial to new elderly lifestyles if it is to be
attractive to potential elderly buyers.

Each segment of the elderly population has its dis-
tinct housing needs. Those in the preretirement age
(55 to 64) and early retirement age (65 to 74) are looking
to maintain their active life and be near friends and

---

[3] It is after the turn of the century, when the
baby boomers begin to enter retirement age, that an explosion
in the elderly population is expected.

Topbound reports are bound at the top of the page. To allow for binding, more space is left at the top. Page numbers are typed at the bottom center of the paper. All other layout guides follow those used for unbound reports.

Layout Guides

1. Top margin: First page, line 12 for pica and line 14 for elite type; succeeding pages, line 10.
2. Side margins, 1"; bottom margin, at least 1".
3. DS the text and indent paragraphs 5 spaces.
4. Main heading: Center in ALL CAPS; if two lines are needed, DS between heading lines; QS below heading to first paragraph.
5. Side heading: Key and underline even with left margin; initial cap main words; DS above and below side heading.
6. Paragraph heading: Indent to paragraph point and underline; follow heading with a period; initial cap *only* the first word of the heading.
7. Enumerated items: SS each item but DS above and below each item. Indent enumerated items

5 spaces from the left margin. Runover lines are blocked at the five-space paragraph indention. This method is more efficient, it improves the ease of readability, and it decreases the possibility of formatting errors.

8. For second and subsequent pages of the report, center and key page number on line 62. Do not number the first page.
9. Textual citations: Place in parentheses; include last name of author(s), year of publication, and page number(s).
10. Reference list: Use main heading "REFERENCES," and QS to first entry. Key list in alphabetic order; SS references, but DS between them; begin first line of each entry at left margin; indent all other lines 5 spaces; place list a QS below last line of report or on a separate page.
11. Title page: Key title of report in ALL CAPS on line 16; initial cap the following: name on line 32; school or department name on line 34; and date on line 50.

CONSUMER PROTECTION   line 16

Carol Ann Farmer   line 32
Northwest Senior High School   line 34

September 1, 19--   line 50

CONSUMER PROTECTION   line 12, pica / line 14, elite

QS

Consumer protection includes all the activities of government, business, and consumer organizations designed to protect consumers' interests as buyers of goods and services. Consumer activism became important in the U.S. around the 1960s. Now, it is important in many other countries. DS

Side Heading   <u>Consumers' Rights</u> DS

The following items are most generally considered consumers' rights:

1. The right to safety from product-related hazards.

2. The right to information about products, including the facts consumers need in order to protect themselves from fraud and misleading product claims.

3. The right to redress, that is, the right to reject unsatisfactory products and services and to obtain satisfaction when the complaint is justified.

4. The right to choose among a variety of products in a marketplace that is free from control by one seller or a few sellers.

5. The right to be heard in governmental decision making that will affect consumers (<u>Academic American Encyclopedia</u>, 1986).

<u>Consumer Protection Development</u>

The U.S. government first became involved in controlling misleading information when a mail fraud law was passed in 1872. One of the first legislations concerning product safety was the Federal Food and Drug Act of 1906, which forbade the adulteration of food and drugs and misbranding.

(at least 1")

ELDERLY HOUSING MARKET

Today, there are more older Americans than ever before, and the number is growing rapidly. Very few elderly people are looking to escape the cold of the North for the warm climate of the Sunbelt. They prefer to stay close to home near family, friends, and familiar services. Therefore, there is a market for elderly housing in all areas of the country. Elderly home buyers demand more than simply shelter. The elderly need environments that will provide them with enjoyable lifestyles.

<u>Demographics of Elderly</u>

The elderly population is loosely defined as those individuals over 55 years old. Persons between 55 and 64 years are included in the elderly market because their housing needs have changed even though many remain active in the labor force.[1]

For years, the elderly have been pictured as being poor,[2] inactive, and in poor health. These perceptions are beginning to change and with good reason. The elderly are not inactive.

---

[1] These individuals are often referred to as "empty nesters" because they no longer have children living at home.

[2] In 1970, one in four elderly people lived in poverty; this is nearly twice the rate for the general population. Today, the poverty rate for the elderly is actually below the overall rate. In per capita terms, median household income is higher for those between 55 and 64 than for any other group. Many elderly are sitting on a gold mine because of the equity in their homes. Nearly 75 percent of those 65 and over own their own homes.

COMMERCIAL BANKS

The most numerous type of bank--commercial bank--originated in its modern form in England and spread to many parts of the world. The U.S. has over 15,000 commercial banks, and their assets total over $1,000 billion.

<u>Functions</u>

Commercial banks, often referred to as full-service banks, offer a full range of services, including:

1. Financing of credit needs--business, consumers, farmers, and government.

2. Receipt of deposits which may be payable on demand or on time.

3. Transfer of funds within the nation in which the bank is located or the transfer of funds between that nation and foreign nations.

4. Issuance of travelers' checks and of letters of credit.

5. Serving as trustee for individuals or corporations.

6. Acting as an agent in the purchasing and selling of securities.

7. Safekeeping of valuables.

8. Dissemination of economic information (<u>Collier's Encyclopedia</u>, 1986).

Commercial banks do offer a wide range of services, most of which involve money in one way or another. A commercial bank is owned by shareholders who buy shares in it. They receive cash dividends from the profits.

If a decision is to be made from a business report, the reader must have confidence in what he or she is reading. Proof is established if all sources that have been quoted or put in the writer's own words are documented.

In order to document reports, source footnotes or discussion footnotes may be used. Source footnotes follow the formal style and refer to references such as books, magazines, or newspapers. Discussion footnotes are more informal and are formatted in sentence style. Discussion footnotes allow the the writer to divert from the main theme and present additional information or comment on the main topic. You will be keying informal, discussion footnotes in this section.

The most conventional location for footnotes is at the bottom of the page on which the reference is cited, although footnotes are sometimes placed at the end of the report. Decisions for footnote construction should be determined and then followed consistently.

Layout Guides

1. Style: Documented business reports are often formatted as leftbound reports so that they can be bound. However, they are sometimes formatted as unbound or topbound reports. In this section, you will be using the leftbound format. If necessary, review the layout guides for leftbound reports on page 27.
2. Footnotes:
   a. To indicate footnotes in the text, use a superior number. If using a typewriter, key the superior number a 1/2 line space above the typing line. If using a word processor, use the proper function key to create a superior number.
   b. Place footnote at the bottom of the same page as the corresponding figure. Footnotes are keyed at the bottom of the page even though the page may be partially filled.
   c. Separate the text and the footnote by a 1 1/2" divider line; DS before and after the divider line.
   d. Indent the first line of each footnote 5 spaces. SS each footnote, but DS between footnotes.

Figure 1 (left): `line 12, elite` / `line 10, pica`

```
                ANNUAL BUDGETS FOR A RETIRED COUPLE
                                QS
     Three hypothetical annual budgets for a retired couple
(husband and wife, age 65 or older) and related cost indexes
have been formulated.  These budgets and cost indexes reflect
the data found in 39 metropolitan areas and have been updated
to indicate the price changes between 1986 and 1987.
     As of September 1987, the estimated, mean annual cost of
the lower-level budget for a retired couple was $5,031.  At the
intermediate and higher levels, the budget cost amounted to
$7,198 and $10,711, respectively.  The following table shows
the three hypothetical budgets:1
```

ANNUAL BUDGETS FOR A RETIRED COUPLE AT THREE LEVELS OF LIVING

Components	Lower Budget	Intermediate Budget	Higher Budget
Total family consumption	$4,814	$6,764	$9,897
Food	1,535	2,035	2,554
Housing	1,745	2,518	3,936
Transportation	337	658	1,215
Clothing and personal care	360	574	868
Medical	628	632	637
Other family consumption	209	347	687
Total other items	217	433	813
Total budget	$5,031	$7,197	$10,710

Source: Bureau of Labor Statistics. **DS**

DS

^{1}Total budget includes the sum of total family consumption and total other items; income taxes are not included.

(at least 1")

Figure 2 (right): `2` `line 6` / `line 8`

```
     The costs represent the 1987 prices of three lists of
goods and services that were specified in the mid-1970s to
portray three levels of living for a retired couple.  The cost
of the lower budget does not represent the income necessary
for subsistence at the poverty level.  These consumption costs
were updated for 1987 by applying the change in the Consumer
Price Index (CPI) between 1986 and 1987 for individual areas
to the 1986 budget costs for each main class of goods and
services.  Changes in consumption costs reflect only changes
in prices.2
     The result of these updates illustrates that between 1985
and 1987, the total cost of the lower budget rose by 4.6
percent, the intermediate by 5.7 percent, and the higher by 6.3
percent.  The total family consumption of the lower, inter-
mediate, and higher budgets rose 5.4 percent, 5.5 percent, and
5.5 percent, respectively; while total other items rose 4.1
percent, 4.3 percent, and 1.4 percent, respectively.  Medical
costs rose over 9 percent for each level due to large cost
increases for all medical services.2
```

DS

^{2}This method of updating is approximate because the CPI reflects spending patterns and prices paid for commodities and services purchased by urban wage earners and clerical workers in general, without regard to their family type or level of living. **DS**

^{3}Because of the time required to compute the budget costs for three levels of living at the required level of disaggregation, the Bureau of Labor Statistics is not able to provide estimates at current price levels.

(at least 1")

Regulations

Commercial banks *in the U.S.* must have a state or federal charter; A *bank* charter is a document granting government permission to establish a bank. *they may choose which they want.*

State-chartered banks. There are over 10,000 state-chartered banks. A state bank may choose whether to join the Federal Reserve System (FRS) *in order to use the system's lending and check-clearing services*. Since 1980 the FRS has the authority to set reserve requirements of all banks (Daughtrey, Ristau, and Eggland, 1986, 235-36). The FRS districts total 12.

Federal-chartered banks. The U.S. has over 4,5000 federally chartered banks or national banks. *National banks must belong to the FRS.* Regulations of national banks are administered by the comptroller of the currency an official of the U.S. Department of the Treasury. National banks must belong to the FRS.

no ¶ The Federal Deposit Insurance Corporation (FDIC) insures the deposits made in nearly all the commercial banks up to $100,000. If an insured bank is unable to give its depositors their money, the FDIC pays up to $100,000 *(Brown and Clow, 1987, 386).*

REFERENCES

"Banking Systems." Collier's Encyclopedia, 1986.

Daughtrey, Anne Scott, Robert A. Ristau, and Steven A. Eggland. Introduction to Business: The Economy and You. Cincinnati: South-Western Publishing Co., 1986.

The choice of a charter determines whether state or federal officials supervise the bank.

Brown, Betty J., and John E. Clow. Our Business and Economic World. 2d ed. Boston: Houghton Mifflin Company, 1987.

used. Polyethylene ~~should~~ *may* be used as a vapor barrier *to cover the ground* where moisture is a problem. *For homes with slab floors, insulation is usually not added due to high installation costs.*

Home Improvement: Walls *Insulation of*

For walls in existing homes, the recommended *insulation* level is R-11. For *of insulating in existing homes* new homes, it is R-19. Blown insulation *(cellulose or fiberglass)* is the most economical way. Be-cause of the difficulty of getting into the ~~walls~~ *existing siding*, a contractor should be hired for this job. ¶ In some cases, *particularly where glass areas are large,* storm windows and doors will reduce heat loss *to the same extent* as insulation ~~does~~ in the ~~attic~~ *walls* *and at a lower cost. Adding storm windows might be a better investment than altering existing siding.*

¶ Whether the job is small or large or whether you are doing it yourself or hiring a contractor, *it is up to you to* make sure you are getting what you pay for.

The insulating materials should be checked before they are installed. Read the *labels* ~~on each~~ package. ~~Does the package give the R-value?~~ *They should give the R-value, as well as the amount you will need for a specific area.*

¶ In addition, make sure you have a reputable company ~~performing~~ *doing* the ~~task~~ *job*. ~~Find out~~ *Ask them for* the names of ~~prior~~ *former* customers you may contact.

¶ If you need more information, please call me (273-6044) at your con-venience or return the attached card. Additional ~~data~~ *information* will be mailed to you immediately. Remember--you ~~can~~ *may* qualify for a home energy loan ~~and~~ *as well as* a discount on your monthly electric bill. Act now!

xx

Enclosure

Job 47 Compose a short memo for your guidance counselor ex-plaining the types of activities you do in each of your classes. Include a general introductory paragraph. Then, using the name of each class as a side heading, explain the different activities you do. In closing, compose a brief summary paragraph. Proofread and correct all errors.

THE ELECTORAL COLLEGE

The Electoral College is the body that elects the presidents and vice presidents of the United States — the only elective federal officials not elected by direct vote of the people. The Electoral College has survived since the founding of the nation despite numerous attempts in Congress to alter or abolish it.

Operation of the College

On presidential election day, the first Tuesday after the first Monday in November of every fourth year, each state chooses as many electors as it has senators and representatives in Congress. Thus, with 100 senators and 435 representatives and 3 electors for the District of Columbia, there are 538 members of the Electoral College, with a majority of 270 electoral votes needed to elect the president and vice president.

Some states print the names of the candidates for president and vice president at the top of the November ballot, while others list only the names of the electors. In either case, the electors of the party receiving the highest vote are elected. The electors meet on the first Monday after the second Wednesday in December in their respective state capitals. They vote for their party nominees. All of the states' electoral votes are then awarded to the winners (<u>Collier's Encyclopedia</u>, 1986). The only Constitutional requirement is that at least one of the persons each elector votes for shall not be an inhabitant of that elector's home state.

 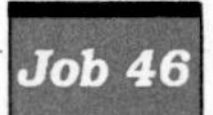 From rough-draft copy, properly format the two-page memo. If using a word processor, recall JOB45; then add corrections that are shown on the rough draft. If neces-sary, move the second-page heading. Save as JOB46. using a word processor, use editing functions.

Line 10 →

TO: Charles ~~Secrest~~ *Povolny*   DS
FROM: Joe T. Murray
DATE: August 17, 19-- *cy*
SUBJECT: Energy Efficient Home*s* *Guidelines*

As a homeowner, you realize the value of maintaining your property. Home improvements, such as adding insulation, can be *easily* translated into savings, *particularly* if you follow *the* energy efficiency guidelines. *for*

¶ Attic ventilation, storm windows and doors, ceiling, wall, and floor in-sulation installed to meet specific standards *often* can ~~help you~~ qualify for a discount on your monthly electric bill.

Insulation of
~~Home Improvement:~~ Attic

The R-number indicates the insulation's ability to keep heat inside in the winter and outside in the sum-mer.

When insulating, start with the attic, ~~because~~ it loses the most heat in your home. It is recommended that an insulation level of R-30 be used for the attic. The higher the R-number, the better the insulation. ¶ If your attic *have insulation of* ~~already has~~ R-11 or more, ~~you should~~ add storm windows and doors, *first* because they represent the next *greatest* ~~best~~ savings.

How much insulation. *Measure the insulation now in the attic.* Try to determine the R-value. Charts are available from *insulation companies* ~~builders~~ to ~~help you find out the R-value;~~ *assist you in determining the R-value.*

Types of insulation. There are many *different* types of insulation on the market. Usually, fiberglass batts or blankets, cellulose, or blown-in wool is used. *for the attic* Each of these insulating materials differs in R-value, *per inch* cost, *flammability,* installation method, *moisture permeability,* and vermin resistance. Consider all these factors. *However, cost and R-value are the most important to consider.*

Installation. In many cases, you will save ~~some~~ money by doing the job yourself. For some types of insulation or in more *complicated* ~~difficult~~ areas, *in your home* hire an insulation contractor. *An insulation contractor can help you determine how much insulation you need.*

Insulation of
~~Home Improvement:~~ Floors

For floors, an R-19 insulation level is recommended. Adding insulation under the floor *can be difficult* ~~is hard~~; however, if the crawl space is adequate, you may be able to do the job yourself. ¶ For wood floors, batt *either or blanket* insulation is

---

Absence of a Majority

Certified and sealed lists of the votes of the electors in each state are mailed to the president of the United States U.S. Senate. He opens them in the presence of the members of the senate and House of Representatives in a joint session held on January 6 (the next day if that day falls on a Sunday), and the electoral votes of all the states are counted.

Proposed Electoral College Changes   by popular vote

There seems to be some fear that direct election would encourage third and fourth parties. It would and also result in the election of a president who received only a minority of the popular vote (World Book Encyclopedia, 1987).

REFERENCES

"Electoral College." Collier's Encyclopedia, 1983 1986.
"Electoral College." World Book Encyclopedia, 1987.

If no candidates for president has a majority, the House of Representatives chooses a president from among the three highest candidates, with all representatives from each state combining to cast one vote for that state. If there are no candidates for vice president, has having a majority, the Senate chooses from the top two,   Center

with the senators voting as individuals

@ 2

under the ceiling and floors [floor] is hard; however, if the crawl space is adequate, do the job yourself. (you may be able to) For wood floors, batt insulation is used. Polyethylene should be used as a vapor barrier where moisture is a problem.

Walls Home Improvement:

[For walls in existing homes, the recommended level is R-16." For new homes, it is R-19. Blown insulation is the most economical way. Because of the difficulty of getting in to the walls, a contractor should be hired for this job. In some cases, storm windows and doors will reduce heat, loss as insulation does in the attic.

[Whether the job is small or large, or whether you are doing it yourself or hiring a contractor, make sure you are getting what you pay for." The insulating materials should be checked before they are used installed. Read the labels on each of the packages. Does the package give the R-value? (¶) In addition, to make sure you have a reputable company performing the task. Find out the names of prior customers who have been satisfied that you may contact or telephone.

(¶) If you need more, information data, please call me at (273-6044) at your convenience or return the attached card. Additional information data will be mailed to you immediately.

(No¶) Remember -- you can qualify for a home energy loan and a discount, on your monthly electric bill. Act now!

xx

Enclosure

COMMERCIAL BANKS

The ~~most numerous type of bank--commercial bank--originated in~~ _commercial bank is the most popular type of bank. It originated in_ its modern form in England and spread to many parts of the world. The U.S. has over 15,000 commercial banks, and their assets total over $1,000 billion.

Functions (Services)

Commercial banks, often referred to as full-service banks, offer a full range of services, including:

1. Financing of credit needs--business, consumers, farmers, and government.

4. Receipt of deposits which may be payable on demand or on time.

3. Transfer of funds within the nation in which the bank is located or the transfer of funds between that nation and foreign nations.

2. Issuance of travelers' checks and of letters of credit.

5. Serving as trustee for individuals or corporations.

7. Acting as an agent in the purchasing and selling of different securities.

6. Safekeeping of valuables.

8. Dissemination of economic information (<u>Collier's Encyclopedia</u>, 1986).

Commercial banks do offer a wide range of services that ~~most of which~~ involve money in one way or another. A commercial bank is owned by shareholders who buy shares in it. They receive cash dividends from the profits.

TO: Charles Secrest
FROM: Joe I. Murray
DATE: August 17, 19--
SUBJECT: ~~Home Improvement~~ Energy Efficient Homes

(¶) As a homeowner, you realize the value of maintaining your property. Home improvements, such as adding insulation, can be translated in to savings if you follow energy efficiency guide lines.

(¶) Attic ventilation, storm windows and doors, ceiling, wall, and floor insulation installed to meet specific standards can help you qualify for a discount on your monthly electric bill because it loses the most heat

Home Improvement: Attic

[When insulating, start with the attic in your home. It is recommended ~~suggested~~ that an insulation level of R-30 for the attic be used. The higher the R-number, the better the insulation. If your attic already has R-11 or more, you should add storm windows and doors because ~~since~~ they represent the next best ~~thing~~ savings.

How much Insulation. Try to determine the R-value. Charts are available from builders to help you find out the R-value.

Types of Insulation. There are Many types of insulation on the market. Usually, fiber glass batts or blankets, cellulose or blown-in wool is used. Each of these insulating materials differs in R-value, cost, installation method, ~~procedure~~ and vermin resistance. Consider all these factors.

Installation. In many ~~some~~ cases, you ~~might~~ will save some money by doing the job yourself. For some types of insulation or in more difficult areas, hire an insulation contractor.

Home Improvement: ~~Ceiling and~~ floors

[For floors, an R-19 insulation level is recommended. Adding insulation

The leftbound report is commonly used in business. This report requires a wider left margin for binding purposes. Because the left and right margins are unequal, a new center point of the typing line must be determined. To calculate the center point, add the left and right margin stops and divide the total by 2. With the exception of the wider left margin and the different center point, the leftbound report follows the same layout as that for the unbound report. See models below.

Layout Guides

1. Top margin: First page, line 10 for pica and line 12 for elite type; succeeding pages, line 8 (with page number on line 6 at right margin).
2. Side margins: Left, 1 1/2"; right, 1". Bottom margin: at least 1".
3. DS the text and indent paragraphs 5 spaces.
4. Main heading: Center in ALL CAPS; if two lines are needed, DS between heading lines; QS below heading to first paragraph.
5. Side heading: Key even with left margin and underline; initial cap main words; DS above and below heading.
6. Paragraph heading: Indent to paragraph point and underline; follow heading with a period; initial cap *only* the first word of the heading.
7. Enumerated items: SS each item, but DS between items. Indent items 5 spaces from left margin. Runover lines are blocked at the five-space paragraph indention.
8. Textual citation: Place in parentheses; include last name of author(s), year of publication, and page number(s).
9. Reference list: Center main heading "REFERENCES" and QS to first entry; key list in alphabetic order; SS references, but DS between them; begin first line of each entry at left margin; indent all other lines 5 spaces; place list a QS below last line of report or on a separate page.
10. Title page: Center title of report in ALL CAPS on line 16; center in initial caps the following: name, line 32; school or department, line 34; and date, line 50.
11. The new center point for leftbound reports is 45 for pica and 54 for elite.

---

line 16   CONSUMER PROTECTION

line 32   Carol Ann Farmer

line 34   Northwest Senior High School

line 50   September 1, 19--

CONSUMER PROTECTION   line 12, elite / line 10, pica

QS

    Consumer protection includes all the activities of government, business, and consumer organizations designed to protect consumers' interests as buyers of goods and services. Consumer activism became important in the U.S. around the 1960s. Now, it is important in many other countries.

Consumers' Rights

    The following items are most generally considered consumers' rights:

    1. The right to safety from product-related hazards.

    2. The right to information about products, including the facts consumers need in order to protect themselves from fraud and misleading product claims.

    3. The right to redress, that is, the right to reject unsatisfactory products and services and to obtain satisfaction when the complaint is justified.

    4. The right to choose among a variety of products in a marketplace that is free from control by one seller or a few sellers.

    5. The right to be heard in governmental decision making that will affect consumers (Academic American Encyclopedia, 1986).

Consumer Protection Development

    The U.S. government first became involved in controlling misleading information when a mail fraud law was passed in 1872. One of the first legislations concerning product safety was the Federal Food and Drug Act of 1906, which forbade the adulteration of food and drugs and misbranding.

(at least 1")

TO: Louis H. Metaxakis

FROM: Felix Sanchez-Boudy

DATE: April 2, 19__

SUBJECT: Long-Term Nursing Care Protection

¶ When you are healthy and active, it is difficult to think about needing the special services of a nursing home or skilled nursing facility. However, it is a health-care option you may need one day. Serious illnesses or injuries occur everyday to people of all ages.

¶ The cost of a long-term stay in a nursing facility can be catastrophic. According to the Health Insurance Association of America, the average cost of a year's stay in a nursing home is as high as $30,000. Most private insurance plans provide limited or no coverage for this type of care. Thus, it would pay to plan ahead with long-term nursing care protection that provides benefits for the following:

1. <u>Nursing home confinement</u>. You can select a daily benefit to meet your personal needs. 2. <u>Hospice care</u>. You are eligible for additional care in a facility or at home. 3. <u>Home health-care service</u>. You are able to receive health care in your home while recuperating from an illness or injury. 4. <u>Home medical alert system</u>. This system can be installed in your home.

¶ In the years ahead, you will recognize the need for this protection. For more information, just complete and return the enclosed postage-paid card. If this new plan is not yet available in your state, you will receive information on the nursing home coverage that is available to you.

Enclosure

STRESS ON THE JOB

Stress is an integral part of everyday life. It cannot be eliminated or avoided. However, it can be reduced and controlled. Stress is simply the physiological reaction to any demand, actual or perceived. Change and challenge create stress. Also, stress is strain or interference that disturbs the proper functioning of an organism (<u>The New Encyclopaedia Britannica</u>, 1987).

<u>Causes of Stress</u>

Stress is becoming increasingly familiar in data processing. The causes of stress vary with each individual. Organizational messages, such as high turnover and absenteeism, may perhaps be the most prevalent of job-related stress markers.

Factors that often increase stress levels include ambiguity, conflict, overload, change, responsibility, and physical conditions. In the data processing profession in particular, job mobility, competition, and the rapid introduction of new technologies and products all create an atmosphere of potentially excessive stress (Owens, 1986, 10).

<u>Coping with Stress</u>

After assessing what alternatives and resources you possess to combat your stress, here are some steps to help you cope with stress: (1) develop a positive attitude, (2) do something nice for yourself and for other people, (3) exercise

<u>Cataract Removal</u> *Methods*

The most modern *up-to-date* methods for cataract removal ~~which~~ *that* are the extra cap-sular and phacoemulsification techniques are used. The *clouded* lens is removed through an *small* incision *using* ultra sound and gentle suction. The posterior cap-sule of the lens is left intact to support the new intra ocular lens im-plant. A highly advanced ultra violet light-filtering intra ocular lens ~~that~~ *,which helps* eliminates any eye problems *is* ~~are~~ used. *that may be associated with harmful ultraviolet light,*

DS>
YAG Laser

DS> Contrary to the belief of some ~~people,~~ the laser can not be used to per-form cataract surgery. A cataract extraction is a surgical procedure requiring *an opening in* ~~surgery on~~ the eye. Occasionally, *however,* the *posterior* capsule of the lens be-come*s* cloudy *after* ~~from~~ cataract surgery *causing decreased* ~~resulting in poor~~ vision. It is at this point that the laser becomes a *valuable* tool in removing this form of *secondary* cataract through a quick ~~and~~ and painless office procedure. A YAG laser is used to make an opening in the center of the *cloudy capsule* ~~eye.~~

<u>Glaucoma Medication</u>

GLAUCOMA *lc* *,which is an increased pressure inside the eye,* is also a major cause of decreased vision among the *elderly* ~~old.~~ If you or some one you know has glaucoma, then you probably know that *glaucoma* ~~it~~ is not only a threat to good vision, but also ~~is~~ a threat to *financial* security due to the high cost of glaucoma medications. (Low-Vision Services)

¶ ~~There are so many people today that~~ have been diagnosed with diseases, such as macular degeneration, optic nerve disease, dia betic retinopathy, or retinal vascular disease, and *they* have been informed that nothing can be done to help them. However, this *is* may not ~~be the case~~ *true* in many cases. With advanced technology and specialists trained *in* providing low vision aid *eye* to patients whose vision *is* ~~has~~ decreased. Many patients improve the quality of their lives by being able to read or to perform other activities ~~that they were not able to perform.~~ ~~Low-vision services are extremely valuable to mod old patients.~~

xx

②

regularly, (4) learn to relax, (5) eat properly, (6)
meditate, and (8) take refuge in family and friends.

<u>Prevention</u>

Many companies are aware of a need to reduce and
prevent such high levels of stress in the work environment.
Some companies have implemented by following policies and
programs: (1) adjusting hours to increase productivity
(flextime), (2) changing lighting to reduce eye stress, (3)
reducing noise, (4) maintaining a constant temperature, and
(5) creating more structured break times, (Hearsch, 1988, 43).

Stress is a problem that has existed and will continue to
exist in our fast-paced environment. Each person encounters
stress to some degree in all professions. The levels of stress and
how it is conrolled vary with every individual. Avoiding stress is
only prolonging the healing process and usually results in mental
and physical impairments. You must have the ability to use stress
to your advantage.

REFERENCES

Hearsch, Robert. "Stress on the Job." <u>Newsweek</u> (April 25,
      1988), 40-45.

Owens, Elizabeth L. "Combatting Stress in the DP
      Environment May Cause Stress." <u>Data Management</u> (December
1986), 10-12.

"Stress." <u>The New Encyclopaedia Britannica</u>, 1987.

TO: Nashwa Abdalla

FROM: Frank C. Mongiarda

Date: *November 24, 19--*

SUBJECT: ~~Eye Care,~~ Cataracts, G*l*aucoma, and Low-Vision Services

Cataracts ~~and glaucoma~~ are the number one ~~reason for~~ *cause of* decreased vision in the U.S. Over two-thirds of the population over *6*0 have ~~an eye~~ *a vision* problem ~~due to~~ *from* cataracts ~~and guaucoma.~~ *Every* ~~Each~~ day, ~~they~~ *cataracts* cause many senior citizens to miss out on the things they enjoy doing, such as reading a book, *doing needlework,* driving a car, and watching *television* ~~TV~~. But with *modern, painless,* highly successful cataract surgery, there's no need to miss out on anything. *Poor vision from cataracts can be improved over 95 percent of the time.*

Cataract Defined

Because reduced vision due to cataracts is usually a gradual process, ~~folks~~ *people* often don't ~~know~~ *realize* how ~~weak~~ *poor* their vision has become, or they explain poor vision as getting old*er*. If you are experiencing any of the following ~~eye~~ problems, then cataracts may ~~indeed~~ be affecting your life:

2. 1. Halos surround objects in bright lights.
   2. ~~Eyes are sensitive to light or glare.~~
   3. Driving is troublesome, particularly at night.
5. 4. Stronger glasses do not improve vision.
4. 5. Reading, sewing, or watching TV are difficult.
1. 6. Vision seems hazy, blurred, or fuzzy; *eyes are sensitive to light and glare.*

DS between enumerated items.

A cataract is a clouding of the *normally clear* lens of the eye ~~eye.~~ It is usually the result of ag*e*ing, but ~~specific~~ *certain* diseases and medications may also cause cataracts. Cataracts prevent light from passing *through* ~~from~~ the lens to the back of the eye or *to* the retina. A cataract causes the light focusing on the retina of your eye to be blurred much like a dirty lens *in a camera would blur the picture taken.*

Cataract Treatment

Once a cataract has been *diagnosed* ~~determined~~, it is up to you to decide how it affects your life and when you should have it removed. The best guideline can *be* to ~~to~~ take ~~no~~ action when the cataract begins to ~~intereres~~ *interfere* with your work or *normal* activities. Cataract micro surgery removes the clouded lens *painlessly* and replaces it with an artificial lens *implant* to restore your vision. *The operation is performed with local anesthesia. It usually takes less than 30 minutes and is done as an outpatient procedure.*

ANCIENT CALENDARS

A calendar is a system of measuring time by dividing time into days, weeks, months, and years. The foundations of a calendric system were constructed around 2000 B.C. when stone circles and alignments were used to determine the solar year length (*Academic American Encyclopedia*, 1986).

Calendar divisions are based on the movements of the earth and appearances of the sun and moon. A day is the average time required for one rotation of the earth on its axis. The measurement of a year is based on one revolution of the earth around the sun and is called a seasonal, tropical, or solar year.

Julian Calendar

The Julian calendar, under which Western nations measured time until 1582 A.D., was authorized by Julius Caesar in 46 B.C. Julius Caesar was advised by the Alexandrian astronomer Sosigenes. The Julian calendar is a solar calendar (not a lunar calendar), and this calendar makes the assumption that the length of the solar year was 365¼ days long. It was announced in 730 A.D. that the 365¼ Julian year was 11 minutes and 14 seconds too long, making a cumulative error of about a day every 128 years. The error had shifted the dates of the seasons. Nothing was done, however, to correct this for over 800 years.

TO: Jack ~~Terrault~~ Jagodzinski

FROM: ~~Tektonidis~~ Alexander (transpose)

DATE: January 27, 19--

SUBJECT: ~~Purchasing Audio Components~~ Understanding Compact Disc Players

Compact disc (CD) players are not ~~unlike~~ any other component in a stereo system. A CD player has more in common with a computer than with a turntable or cassette deck. CD players use a laser to read the disc's microscopic pits which represent the binary digits or bits of digitally en coded music. The three-beam pick up system doesn't have (3) separate beams but a single beam of laser light split three ways. The middle beam reads the data, while the leading and trailing beams monitor the position of the pickup in relation to adjacent tracks. This system keeps the main beam properly tracking.

Early CD players used filters (analog). The state-of-the-art machines use advanced digital circuits that filter out unwanted noise before the signal is converted back to analog. Computer technology has made possible sound quality and convenience features that would have seemed like science fiction until recently. Compact disc players are leading this revolution, providing "you-are-there" sound quality.

A CD is read as a stream of sequential bits of data. If a portion of the stream is missing or corrupted, so will be the music. As the stream of data is read, each sample is compared with the one before and the one that follows. Too great a difference between samples indicates an error. By knowing what comes before and after the error, the CD player's "brain" can inter polate what's missing and fill in the gap. This error correction circuitry is so exceptional that even damaged discs can usually be played without degraded sound quality.

Now is an exciting time to be shopping for audio components, especially CDs.

xx

2

<u>Gregorian Calendar</u>

¶ By 1582, the accumulated error was estimated to have amounted to 10 days from Caesar's time. In that year, Pope Gregory XIII decreed that the day following October 4, 1582, should be called October 15, thus dropping 10 days. The Julian calendar was gradually abandoned in favor of the Gregorian calendar (*The New Encyclopaedia Britannica*, 1987).

The Gregorian calendar or New Style calendar was slowly adoped throughout Europe. It is used today throughout most of the Western world and in parts of Asia.

¶ However, with common years 365 days and a 366-day leap year every fourth year, the error in the length of the year would have recurred at the rate of a little more than three days every 400 years. Thus, 1600 was a leap year, but 1700, 1800, and 1900 were common years. So three out of every four centesimal years were made common years, not leap years. Leap years are those divisible by four except centesimal years, which are common unless divisible by 400. ¶

REFERENCES

"Calendar." *Academic American Encyclopedia*, 1986.

"Julian Calendar." *The New Encyclopaedia Britannica*, 1987.

Job 40 Key the full-page memo below from rough draft. Follow the layout guides on page 61. If using a word processor, recall JOB39; then edit as shown on the rough draft.

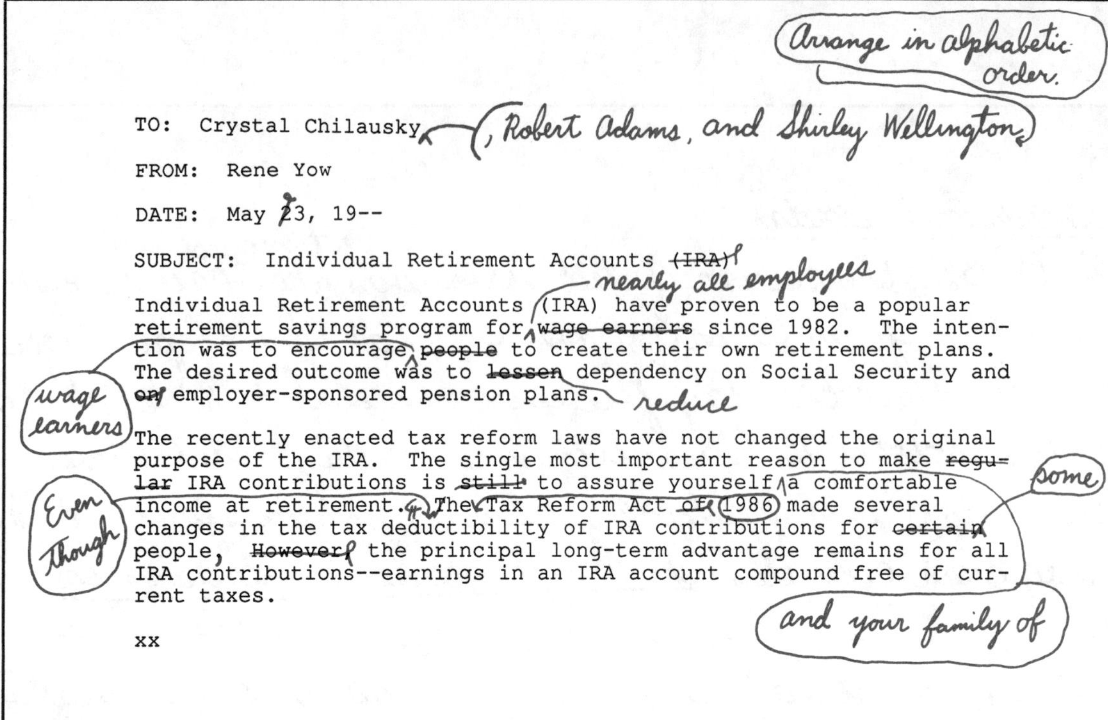

Job 41 Prepare the full-page memo shown below from script. Include your reference initials. Proofread and correct errors. If using a word processor, use editing functions.

TO: Fred Thompson
FROM: Bennie Bertalot
DATE: October 11, 19--
SUBJECT: Integrated Services Digital Network (ISDN)

(¶) Can you imagine calling home to raise or lower the temperature or to check on your burglar alarm? Well, it is now a reality. The technology that will make these types of services possible took a giant step forward last month when our company began offering the nation's first multicustomer application of the telecommunications technology of the future.

(¶) The new technology, known as Integrated Services Digital Network (ISDN), can take spoken conversation and a data transmission and transmit them digitally over the same telephone line. It is this type of transmission that may someday allow you to call home and control your appliances or home monitoring system.

(¶) The ISDN application is being offered now on a limited basis by a $3.7 million switching system located in Dallas. This system offers ISDN services to multiple customers on an ongoing basis.

STRESS ON THE JOB

Stress is an integral part of everyday life. It cannot
be eliminated or avoided. However, it can be reduced and controlled. Stress is ~~simply~~ the physiological reaction to any
demand, actual or perceived. Change ~~and~~ as well as challenge can create
stress. ~~Also,~~ stress is defined as the strain or interference that disturbs
the proper functioning of an organism (<u>The New Encyclopaedia
Britannica</u>, 1987).

<u>Causes of Stress</u>

Stress is becoming increasingly familiar in the area of data processing. The causes of stress vary with each individual. Organizational messages, such as high turnover and absenteeism, may
~~perhaps~~ be the most prevalent of job-related stress markers.

Factors that often increase stress levels include ambiguity, conflict, ~~overload,~~ change, responsibility, and physical
conditions. In the data processing profession in particular,
job mobility, competition, and the rapid introduction of new
technologies and products all create an atmosphere of potentially excessive stress (Owens, 1986, 10).

<u>Coping with Stress</u>

After assessing what alternatives and resources you pos-
sess to combat your stress, here are some ~~steps to~~ ways that will help you
cope with stress: (1) develop a positive attitude, (2) do
something nice for yourself and for ~~other~~ people, (3) exercise

Interoffice memorandums, commonly called memos, are informal messages. A memo informs, requests, or recommends. The message should be straightforward and brief. Any employee may originate a memo.

The company usually provides a simple, standard form which includes the printed headings TO, FROM, DATE, and SUBJECT. The use of courtesy titles (Mr., Mrs., etc.) and the use of job titles (Office Manager, etc.) with the sender's or receiver's name is optional. Variations in size and color of forms may be used by different departments. A form that is simply designed will permit the message to be formatted quickly and accurately. A copy of each memo should be made for the files.

Layout Guides

The following guides represent one acceptable form for preparing memorandums:

1. Begin heading information 2 spaces to the right of printed headings. If printed forms are not available, format the headings as shown in the model below.

2. Top margin: half sheet, line 6; full sheet, line 10.
3. 1" side margins; approximately 1" bottom margin.
4. SS the message; DS above and below paragraphs.
5. DS between the subject and message.
6. SS enumerated items; DS above and below enumerated items. Block run-over lines at the left margin.
7. DS below message to reference initials.
8. If appropriate, include a carbon copy notation (cc), a photocopy notation (pc), or an enclosure line.
9. Second-page heading is keyed at the left margin.
   a. Key addressee on line 6.
   b. Key "Page" and page number on line 7.
   c. Key current date on line 8.
   d. DS below date before continuing the memo.

Following is an example of a second page heading:

Line 6 ⟶ Lucy Parker
Line 7 ⟶ Page 2
Line 8 ⟶ Current date

Job 39 Key the following memo as shown, following layout guides. If using a word processor, save as JOB39.

Proofread and correct errors. If using a word processor, use editing functions.

```
TO:   Crystal Chilausky   line 6
                     DS
FROM:   Rene Yow  DS

DATE:   May 23, 19--  DS

SUBJECT:   Individual Retirement Accounts (IRA) DS

Individual Retirement Accounts (IRA) have proven to be a popular
retirement savings program for wage earners since 1982.  The inten-
tion was to encourage people to create their own retirement plans.
The desired outcome was to lessen dependency on Social Security and
on employer-sponsored pension plans. DS

The recently enacted tax reform laws have not changed the original
purpose of the IRA.  The single most important reason to make regu-
lar IRA contributions is still to assure yourself a comfortable
income at retirement.  The Tax Reform Act of 1986 made several
changes in the tax deductibility of IRA contributions for certain
people.  However, the principal long-term advantage remains for all
IRA contributions--earnings in an IRA account compound free of cur-
rent taxes.

xx
```

1" (left margin)   1" (right margin)

(at least 1")

2

regularly, (4) learn to relax, (5) eat properly, (6) meditate, and (7) take refuge in family and friends.

<u>Prevention</u> *Measures*

Businesses are aware of the need to reduce and prevent such high levels of stress in the work environment. Some companies have implemented the following policies and programs: (1) adjust hours to increase productivity (flextime), (2) create more structured break times, (3) reduce noise, (4) change lighting to reduce eye stress, and (5) maintain a constant temperature (Hearsch, 1988, 43).

Stress is a problem that has existed and will continue to exist in our fast-paced environment. Every person *faces* ~~encounters~~ stress to some degree in all *jobs* ~~professions~~. Avoiding stress is only prolonging the healing process and ~~usually~~ results in mental and physical impairments. ~~The levels of stress and how it is controlled vary with every individual,~~ You must have the ability to use stress to your advantage.

REFERENCES

Hearsch, Robert. "Stress on the Job." <u>Newsweek</u> (April 25, 1988), 40-45.

Owens, Elizabeth L. "Combatting Stress in the DP Environment May Cause Stress." <u>Data Management</u> (December 1986), 10-12.

"Stress." <u>The New Encyclopaedia Britannica</u>, 1987.

Betsy T. Bluethenthal; *Jerry King, Jr.; and Glenn Wise*
Page 2
Current date

cards that charge you annual fees and require *high* monthly payments, ~~that are very high,~~ Be sure to indicate the amount of cash advance you need on your Membership Request Certificate.

~~The Executive Choice Card with no fees and a $25,000 credit line is exceptional. Complete the Membership Request Certificate that is attached and return it to us in the stamped envelope.~~

Your $25,000 Executive Choice Card and immediate cash advance are available now, but only through the date on your Membership Request Certificate. Return your completed certificate today.

Mary Alice Timberlake
Vice President *Senior*

xx

Enclosures

The Executive Choice Card with no annual fees and a $25,000 Credit line is an exceptional value. Complete the Membership Request Certificate that is enclosed and return it to us in the Postage-paid envelope provided.

Job 38 Compose a simplified memo to your principal, parents, or teacher listing four of your best strengths as an individual. Then list several of your areas needing improvement. Edit the memo. Prepare a final copy.

Section F REPORTS WITH OUTLINE, FOOTNOTES, AND BIBLIOGRAPHY

The purpose of a formal report is to make a careful study of a topic. You must interpret and present the material in an organized and logical manner.

To increase the effectiveness of the report, limit the topic before starting to collect information. It is also useful to develop one sentence that states the purpose of the report. Then develop an outline by dividing your basic topic into its parts. This outline may change as data are collected, but it helps the writer eliminate unnecessary information.

Put together in you own words the information that has been collected. If you quote directly or use another persons ideas, give proper credit by footnoting this information. Avoid using too many direct quotations. Take care to record source information accurately and make certain that footnotes are formatted correctly.

The final page of the report is the bibliography. The bibliography identifies the books, articles, or other sources used in constructing the report. A bibliography should contain all sources examined whether or not they were cited in the body of the report.

Layout Guides

1. Style: Formal reports are usually typed as a leftbound report. If necessary, review the layout guides for leftbound reports listed on page 27.
2. Footnotes:
   a. To indicate footnotes in the text, use a superior number. If using a typewriter, key the superior number a 1/2 line space above the typing line. If using a word processor, use the proper function key to create a superior number.
   b. Place footnote at the bottom of the same page as the corresponding figure. Footnotes are keyed at the bottom of the page even though the page may be partially filled.
   c. Separate the text and the footnote by a 1 1/2" divider line; DS before and after the divider line.
   d. Indent the first line of each footnote 5 spaces. SS each footnote, but DS between footnotes.
3. Quotations: Use quotation marks to set off short quotations. Long quotations (4 lines or more) are SS and indented 5 spaces from the left margins. The omission of words from a quotation is called ellipses. They are keyed by alternating 3 spaces and periods (. . .) or 4 spaces (. . . .) if the end of a sentence period is included in the omission.
4. Bibliography: List each entry in alphabetic order. Indent second and succeeding lines 5 spaces. SS each entry, but DS between them.
5. Title Page and Outline: See models below.

line 16 HISTORICAL FOUNDATIONS OF MUSICAL TASTE

line 32 Trelles Glenn Case

line 34 Lincoln Senior High School

line 50 March 11, 19--

line 10, pica
line 12, elite HISTORICAL FOUNDATIONS OF MUSICAL TASTE QS

2 spaces

I. INTRODUCTION ← ALL CAPS
   A. Musical Taste of Individuals ← Initial Cap
   B. Definitions of Musical Taste
      1. Seashore's definition ← Cap 1st Word
      2. Mueller's definition
DS
II. CULTURE AND MUSICAL TASTE
DS
   A. Culture and Music Preferences
   B. Research Studies of Musical Behavior
      1. Farnsworth study
      2. Lundin study
DS
1 1/2" → III. MUSICAL TASTE FACTORS
DS
   A. Conditioning
      1. Function of musical taste
      2. Tempo preference and job activity
   B. Training
      1. Effects of training on musical taste
      2. Knowledge of musical form

5. Worldwide travel accident insurance of $750,000.

6. Rebate of 1 percent on all purchases made with your Executive Choice Card.

Current date

Betsy T. Bluethenthal; *Add these names: Jerry King, Jr.; and Glenn Wise*

EXECUTIVE CHOICE CARD

As you have ~~an~~ *see* excellent credit record, you have been ~~carefully~~ selected to ~~hear about~~ the special privileges of the $25,000 Executive Choice Card. This card was designed to provide appropriate *other* levels of ~~economic~~ *financial* security, "clout," and flexibility that no ~~credit~~ card ~~on the market now~~ can match. *currently available*

Here Executive Choice Card is a ~~premier~~ card that *can* separates you from your peers! ~~The following~~ are ~~just~~ a few of the ~~primary~~ benefits ~~that~~ this card provides:

1. <u>Credit line of $25,000</u>. This credit line is much higher than ~~most other~~ credit lines offered by most banks.

2. <u>No annual fees</u>. This benefit *alone* can save you and your ~~friends~~ *colleagues* hundreds of dollars annually. — *Use the card any way you prefer.*

3. <u>Immediate cash advance</u>. When you become an Executive Choice cardholder, we will automatically send you a cash advance check. Unlike most credit cards, this card allows you immediate cash. Just check the amount of cash advance you desire on the Membership Request Certificate.

4. <u>Airline tickets or $3,000 emergency cash</u>. You will be ~~able~~ *entitled* to *get* ~~obtain~~ a cash advance at over 199,500 bank offices or through more than 35,750 automated teller machines worldwide. If you misplace *arrange* your card, call the toll-free number immediately. We will ~~send you~~ up to $3,000 cash or prepaid airline tickets so that your ~~vacation will not be interrupted~~. *trip will not be interrupted.*

The *enclosed brochure* ~~attached bulletin~~ gives more *complete* details on ~~the~~ *each of* ~~invaluable~~ benefits ~~listed above as well as on the following benefits:~~ *Additional benefits include:*

1. Free checking—unlimited.

2. No transaction fees.

3. Automobile rental collision protection of $50,000. (Most companies charge at least $25 per day for this service.)

4. One or more additional cards without charge.

Your Executive Choice Card and *immediate* cash advance are available only together. Why not use it to pay off the balances of your other

5. <u>Low monthly payments</u>. Your minimum monthly payments will be just 5 percent of your outstanding balance.

Main Heading   HISTORICAL FOUNDATIONS OF MUSICAL TASTE   QS

1 1/2"   The musical taste of individuals and groups is just like
any other form of social behavior. To understand the nature
of musical taste, a general, empirical frame of reference must   1"
be established. However, a canvass of various references would
lead one to believe that there is no authoritative definition
of musical taste.[1]

    Seashore has defined musical taste as "a sort of general
indicator of musical feeling. But taste in music, like good
taste in other things, is a somewhat elusive factor."[2] Using
an empirical approach, Mueller asserted that musical taste is
"the more or less consistent range of aesthetic preference by
a given group. . . ."[3]   DS

Side   Culture and Musical Taste   DS
Heading
    According to Farnsworth's research, musical taste is cul-
turally derived.[4] Studies of musical behavior conducted by
Farnsworth and Meyer in cultures other than the United States   DS

————————   DS

[1]Paul R. Farnsworth, _The Social Psychology of Music_ (New
York: The Dryden Press, 1958), p. 116.   DS

[2]Carl E. Seashore, _The Psychology of Musical Talent_ (Boston: Silver, Burdett and Company, 1919), p. 268.

[3]John H. Mueller, "Methods of Measurement of Aesthetic
Folkways," _The American Journal of Sociology_ (January 1946),
p. 276.

[4]Farnsworth, p. 119.

(at least 1")

---

line 8   have found individual differences in the kinds of music and   line 6 2
preferences for music. These findings provide evidence that
musical preferences are not universal but are influenced by
many aspects of the specific culture.[5] Additional evidence
supporting this is demonstrated in the following anthropologi-
cal research data: DS

Indent 5   It has been shown that the Occidental love for simple
spaces from   rhythms, careful tuning, fixed tonal steps, harmonies,
left margin.   the tonic effect, and the diatonic scale is not shared
        the world over. . . . The African predilection for com-
        plicated rhythmic patterns was so far out of line with
        the taste and perceptual abilities of many of the early
        missionaries that they commonly reported the Africans to
        be arhythmical. The Chinese often appear oblivious to
        mistunings; they love music which has little harmony
        in the Western sense of the word. Yet Orientals can
        learn to love Occidental music and, indeed, with con-
        tinued residence in America come to appreciate Western
        musical principles, and gradually to develop facility in
        the perception of small auditory differences. Conversely,
        the people of the Western world often learn to love alien
        music forms, and to master more complicated rhythmic
        patterns. When constantly subjected to poor tuning, the
        American slowly loses his pitch sensitivity and his need
        for pitch exactitude.[6] DS

Side   Factors of Musical Taste DS
Heading
    A review of selected references reveals that there are
numerous factors that influence the formation of musical taste.
Factors that are mentioned most frequently include conditioning, training, repetition and familiarity, age, as well as
intelligence. DS

———————— DS

[5]Robert W. Lundin, _An Objective Psychology of Music_ (New
York: The Ronald Press Company, 1967), p. 182.

[6]Farnsworth, pp. 119-120.

(at least 1")

Paragraph   line 6 3
Heading   _Conditioning_. Likes and dislikes are frequently associated with pleasant and unpleasant stimuli. A composition
may be liked or disliked because of its particular association
with a stimulus. This concept of conditioning is a function
of musical taste.[7]

    In the area of tempo, it has been determined that there
is a relationship between the pace of the job activity and the
musical tempo preference of the subject in various trades.[8]
Relativity of musical taste is culture-bound, not culture-
free.[9]

    Training. Kingsley[10] has researched the effects of musi-
cal training on musical taste. He agrees that having musical
training or education is definitive in determining an individual's taste.

————————   DS

[7]Lundin, p. 188.

[8]John P. Foley, Jr. "The Occupational Conditioning of
Preferential Auditory Tempo," _Journal of Social Psychology_
(August 1940), pp. 121-129.

[9]Farnsworth, pp. 152-153.

[10]H. L. Kingsley, _The Nature and Conditions of Learning_
(Englewood Cliffs: Prentice-Hall, Inc., 1946), p. 426.

(at least 1")

---

line 10, pica   line 6 4
line 12, elite   BIBLIOGRAPHY   QS

Farnsworth, Paul R. _The Social Psychology of Music_. New York:
    The Dryden Press, 1958. DS
Foley, John P., Jr. "The Occupational Conditioning of Prefer-
    ential Auditory Tempo." _Journal of Social Psychology_,
    August 1940, 121-129.
Kingsley, H. L. _The Nature and Conditions of Learning_.
1 1/2"   Englewood Cliffs: Prentice-Hall, Inc., 1946.
Lundin, Robert W. _An Objective Psychology of Music_. New York:
    The Ronald Press Company, 1967.
Mueller, John H. "Methods of Measurement of Aesthetic Folk-
    ways." _The American Journal of Sociology_, January 1946,
    276.
Seashore, Carl E. _The Psychology of Musical Talent_. Boston:
    Silver, Burdett and Company, 1919.

be interrupted. 2

(¶) The attached bulletin gives more details on the invaluable benefits listed above as well as on the following benefits:

1. Free checking unlimited.
2. No transaction fees.
3. Automobile rental collision protection of $50,000. (Most companies charge at least $25 per day for this service.)
4. One or more additional cards without charge.

(¶) Your Executive Choice Card and cash advance are available only together. Why not use it to pay off the balances of your other cards that charge you annual fees and require monthly payments that are very high. Be sure to indicate the amount of cash advance you need on your Membership Request Certificate.

(¶) The Executive Choice Card with no fees and a $25,000 credit line is exceptional. Complete the Membership Request Certificate that is attached and return it to us in the stamped envelope.

(¶) Your $25,000 Executive Choice Card and immediate cash advance are available now, but only through the date on your Membership Request Certificate. Return your completed certificate today.

Mary Alice Timberlake
Vice President
xx
Enclosures

 Using the model below and following the layout guides on page 34, key the outline.   Proofread and correct all errors.

If using a word processor, save the document as Job22.

```
           ELECTRONIC DATA INTERCHANGE IN THE TEXTILE INDUSTRY


      I.   NEW INFORMATION TECHNOLOGY IN THE MARKETPLACE

           A.  Point-of-Sale (POS) Terminals
           B.  Electronic Data Interchange (EDI)
           C.  Traditional Approach to Consumer Demands
                1.  Unscientific estimates of trends
                2.  Production-oriented markets
           D.  Information Technology Approach to Consumer Demands
                1.  POS devices
                2.  Consumer-oriented market
                3.  Manufacturer trends

      II.  CONCEPT OF ELECTRONIC DATA INTERCHANGE

           A.  Telecommunications Technology
                1.  Data transferred electronically
                2.  Orders confirmed
                3.  Shipping documents transmitted electronically
           B.  Applications
```

Current date
Betsy T. Bluethenthal
EXECUTIVE CHOICE CARD
(¶) As you have an excellent credit record, you have been carefully selected to hear about the special privileges of the $25,000 Executive Choice Card. This card was designed to provide appropriate levels of economic security, "clout," and flexibility that no credit card on the market now can match.
(¶) Executive Choice Card is a premier card that separates you from your peers! The following are just a few of the primary benefits that this card provides:

1. Credit line of $25,000. This credit line is much higher than most other credit lines offered by most banks.

2. No annual fees. This benefit can save you and your friends hundreds of dollars annually.

3. Immediate cash advance. When you become an Executive Choice cardholder, we will automatically send you a cash advance check. Unlike most credit cards, this card allows you immediate cash. Just check the amount of cash advance you desire on the Membership Request Certificate.

4. Airline tickets or $3,000 emergency cash. You will be able to obtain a cash advance at over 199,500 bank offices or through more than 35,750 automated teller machines worldwide. If you misplace your card, call the toll-free number immediately. We will send you up to $3,000 cash or prepaid airline tickets so that your vacation will not

ELECTRONIC DATA INTERCHANGE IN THE TEXTILE INDUSTRY

<u>New Information Technology</u>

New information technology is bringing about sweeping changes in the way domestic textile manufacturers are doing business. Point-of-sale terminals (POS) and electronic data interchange (EDI), a form of electronic mail,[1] have revolutionized the flow of information in the industry. Production managers are becoming aware of the new information available to them, and they are applying this information to improve the efficiency of their operations.

Producers of textiles have had to rely heavily on unscientific estimates of consumer demands. Predictions of future consumer trends were based on the opinions of style and fashion experts. If the experts were wrong, however, the negative impact on manufacturers with resources dedicated to producing unpopular goods was tremendous. As a result, the industry leaned towards a production-oriented mind-set. Emphasis was placed on large production runs (to reduce unit costs)[2] using readily available raw materials. If the produced goods were unpopular with the consumer, then inventories backed up.

---

[1]"Electronic Mail, One Decade Old," <u>The Wall Street Journal</u>, 27 May 1987, p. 1.

[2]N. Allen Hunter, "How to Make Quick Response Work for You," <u>Textile World</u> (May 1986), pp. 54-55.

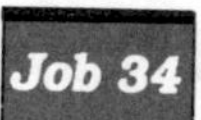

Prepare the following half-page memo from script. Refer to the layout guides, page 53. Add reference initials. If using a word processor, save as JOB34 and print one copy. Proofread and correct all errors.

Current date

Unicom Bell Customers

DIALING LONG-DISTANCE TELEPHONE CALLS

(¶) The least expensive way to place a Unicom Bell long-distance call is to dial direct. Unicom Bell provides long-distance service within the boundaries of your calling zone. Calls to destinations outside your calling zone are handled by companies other than Unicom Bell.

(¶) Direct-dialed telephone calls are placed without any assistance from the operator. To dial directly, just dial 1 plus the area code (if different from yours) plus the seven-digit telephone number you are calling.

Anna R. Mendez

Customer Service Manager

Job 35

From the corrected script copy below, key the memo. Add reference initials. If using a word processor, save as JOB35 and print one copy. Then key a one-page memo combining JOB35 and JOB36. (New editing function: **define, move**)

Current date   (Unicom Bell Customers

DIALING LONG-DISTANCE TELEPHONE CALLS

(¶) For operator-assisted calls, Unicom has ~~several~~ three types. Each ~~of the following~~ types can be made by dialing O plus the area code plus the seven-digit number you ~~desire~~ are calling. (DS)

1. _Collect._ When the operator is on the line, request a collect call and state your full name.

3 2. _Third-number billed call._ When the operator is on the line ~~answers,~~ request the call to be billed to a third number. ~~Then,~~ give the operator the number to which you are billing the call.

2 3. _Person-to-person._ When the operator is on the line, request a person-to-person call and state the name of the person with whom you wish to speak.

(¶) If you need help, dial the operator for assistance.

Anna R. ~~Pierce~~ Mendez

Customer Service Manager

2

Considerable losses were incurred as markdowns were employed to move unwanted inventory.

In recent years, retailers have relied increasingly on electronic point-of-sale devices to record sales and control inventory levels. Information gathered daily from POS is used to prepare purchase orders and restock store shelves. There are now enough POS terminals in retail stores across the country to act as the much-needed monitor of consumer demand. Retailers are now receiving daily feedback about consumer preferences that used to take weeks or even months to collect.

Clothing producers are receiving this new consumer demand information in the form of purchase orders from retailers. In time, textile manufacturers will also feel the influence of the improved information flow as new orders are placed by their customers.

Now, manufacturers are able to produce smaller and more marketable inventories that turn faster and require fewer markdowns. For example, Levi Strauss reported a drop in days of inventory from one month to a three-day supply after implementing EDI.[3] Lead times on production orders have shrunk from more than a month to less than a week in many such manufacturing cases.

---

[3] David Wessel, "Computer Finds a Role in Buying and Selling, Reshaping Business." _The Wall Street Journal_, 16 October, 1986, 1.

Current date

Stockholders

NOTICE OF ANNUAL MEETING OF STOCKHOLDERS

Notice is hereby given that the Annual Meeting of Stockholders of Universal Corporation will be held on ~~the third~~ Tuesday, ~~of~~ March 22, 19--, on the second floor of the Universal National Building at 1600 Peachtree Street, Atlanta, Georgia, at ~~11:00 A.M.~~ 10:30 ~~(local time)~~ for the following purposes:

1. To fix the number of directors at 25.

2. To elect ~~four~~ five directors for a three-year term.

3. To approve a stock option proposal for nonemployee directors and associate directors.

4. To name independent auditors.

6. To transact such other business as may properly come before the meeting or any adjournment thereof.

The board of directors has fixed March 3, 19--, as the record date for the determination of stockholders entitled to receive notice of and to vote at the annual meeting. Also, stockholders are advised that "Form F-2, Annual Report," is available for review at Universal Corporation, 1600 Peachtree Street, Atlanta, GA 30303-2234.

It is ~~important~~ essential that your shares of the corporation's common stock be represented at this meeting to assure the presence of a quorum. ~~Therefore,~~ please sign, date, and return the enclosed proxy, whether or not you ~~expect~~ do attend the meeting in person. If you attend, your proxy will be returned to you upon request.

Charles R. Edwards, Secretary

xx

Enclosures: Proxy and Envelope

Only stockholders of record at the close of business on that date will be entitled to notice of and to vote at said annual meeting.

5. To authorize the board of directors to purchase or cause to be purchased on behalf of the corporation up to 500,000 shares of common stock of the corporation.

3

[<u>Concept of Electronic Data Interchange</u>

Manufacturers of textiles have been turning to EDI technology for answers. Just as POS terminals are ~~often~~ used to gather information at the consumer level, EDI is the information system used at the retail ^and^ manufacturing levels. Studies show that approximately 70 per cent of one computer's out put is another computer's input, and 25 percent of transaction costs ^are^ caused by manual data entry.[4]

<u>Applications</u>. Current applications of EDI, ^have been well^ ~~has been~~ received by both the suppliers and their customers. Customers receive better service, and producers find that they are more competitive. Paper flow is ~~seldom~~ reduced and information bottle necks are eliminated.

<u>Telecommunications technology</u>. EDI relies ^upon^ telecommunications technology to link the (customer's) computer directly to the supplier's computer. Purchase orders are transmitted electronically to the supplier. Once the computers are able to communicate, ~~the~~ bottlenecks caused by conventional paper flows can be ~~removed~~ eliminated.

---

[4] McAllister Issacs, III, "Electronic Communication Cuts JIT Paperwork Flow," <u>Textile World</u> (December 1986), pp. 47-57.

Current date

Stockholders

NOTICE OF ANNUAL MEETING OF STOCKHOLDERS

Notice is hereby given that the Annual Meeting of Stockholders of Universal Corporation will be held on the third Tuesday of March, 19--, on the second floor of the Universal National Building at 1600 Peachtree Street, Atlanta, Georgia, at 11:00 A.M. (local time) for the following purposes:

1. To elect four directors for a three-year term.

2. To approve a stock option proposal for nonemployee directors and associate directors.

3. To name independent auditors.

4. To transact such other business as may properly come before the meeting or any adjournment thereof.

Stockholders
Page 2
Current date

The board of directors has fixed March 1, 19--, as the record date for the determination of stockholders entitled to receive notice of and to vote at the annual meeting. Also, stockholders are advised that "Form F-2, Annual Report," is available for review at Universal Corporation, 1600 Peachtree Street, Atlanta, GA 30303-2234.

It is important that your shares of the corporation's common stock be represented at this meeting to assure the presence of a quorum. Therefore, please sign, date, and return the enclosed proxy, whether or not you expect to attend the meeting in person. If you attend, your proxy will be returned to you.

Charles R. Edwards, Secretary

xx

Enclosures: Proxy and Envelope

4

BIBLIOGRAPHY

"Electronic Mail, One Decade Old." <u>The Wall Street Journal</u>,
     27 May 1987, 1.

Hunter, N. Allen. "How to Make Quick Response Work for You."
     <u>Textile World</u> (May 1986), 54-55.

Issacs, McAllister, III. "Electronic Communication Cuts JIT
     Paperwork Flow." <u>Textile World</u> (December 1986), 47-57.

Wessel, David. "Computer Finds a Role in Buying and Selling,
     Reshaping Business." <u>The Wall Street Journal</u>, 16 October
     1986, 1.

Job 25 Using the information listed below and the layout guides on page 34, key a title page. If using a word processor, use editing functions. Save as JOB25.

Title: ELECTRONIC DATA INTERCHANGE IN THE TEXTILE INDUSTRY
Name: Carl Benjamin Artinger
School: E. E. Smith Senior High
Date: April 1, 19--

A memorandum is a formatted report designed to send, record, or confirm information. Simplified memorandum reports are processed on plain paper or letterhead paper, while formal/traditional memorandum reports are processed on printed forms that use the headings: TO, FROM, DATE, and SUBJECT.

A simplified, informal memorandum may take the form of an announcement of a meeting or a new product, or it may contain a list of customers to be contacted. Length and arrangement have very little to do with the contents. The headings (TO, FROM, DATE, and SUBJECT) are not included.

Layout Guides

The following guides represent one acceptable form for formatting memorandums:

1. Top margin: half sheet, line 6 (5 blank lines); full sheet, line 10 (9 blank lines).
2. Use 1" side margins and approximately 1" bottom margins.
3. QS below the dateline.
4. DS below the addressee to the subject line.
5. DS below the subject line to the body.
6. SS the body; DS between paragraphs.
7. QS below last paragraph to writer's name.
8. DS below writer's name to reference initials.
9. If appropriate, DS below reference initials to copy notation or enclosure notation.
10. Second-page heading is placed at left margin.
    a. Key addressee on line 6.
    b. Key "Page" and page number on line 7.
    c. Key current date on line 8.
    d. DS below the date before continuing the memorandum.
11. Enumerated items: Block all lines at left margin; DS above and below enummerated items.

April 14, 19--   **line 10**

    QS

Dorothy A. Gibbs, Robert Hartman, and Gloria G. Pons **DS**

ANNUITY OPTION SELECTION **DS**

You should begin considering the annuity options available to you before you need the retirement income. You first must determine which portion of your account you would like to annuitize.

You may decide to receive annuity payments on the total amount of your accumulated funds. You may also wish to receive annuity payments on a portion of your accumulated funds and leave the balance in your account to continue earning interest or investment earnings on a tax-deferred basis, subject to applicable IRS distribution requirements. Keep in mind that if you are under age 59 1/2 and elect a partial annuitization, the annuitized amount may be subject to a 10% federal penalty tax. A total annuitization of your account is not generally subject to this penalty.

Review the following annuity options available to you and determine which option or combination of options suits your retirement income needs: **DS**

1. Single life annuity. Guarantees you will receive income for life. **DS**

2. Life annuity with 60, 120, 180, or 240 monthly payments guaranteed. Guarantees you will receive income for life. If you die before payments have been made for 60, 120, 180, or 240 months as selected, annuity payments will continue to your beneficiary during the remaining guaranteed period of time.

3. Payments for designated period. Through a series of monthly payments over a specific, selected period of time, you liquidate your account. If you die before all payments are made, the remaining payments will be made to your beneficiary. **DS**

Please call my office soon to discuss your annuity option selection.

    QS

Nicholas W. Patella, Annuity Supervisor

xx   **DS**

ELECTRONIC DATA INTERCHANGE ~~IN THE~~ TEXTILE INDUSTRY:

MARKET TECHNOLOGY CHANGING

I. ~~NEW INFORMATION TECHNOLOGY IN THE MARKETPLACE~~

    A. Point-of-Sale (POS) Terminals
    B. Electronic Data Interchange ~~(EDI)~~
    C. Traditional Approach ~~to~~ Consumer Demands:
        1. ~~Unscientific~~ estimates of trends
        2. Production-oriented markets
    D. Information Technology Approach ~~to~~ Consumer Demands:
        1. POS devices
        2. Consumer-oriented markets
        3. Manufacturer trends

EDI CONCEPTS

II. ~~CONCEPTS OF ELECTRONIC DATA INTERCHANGE~~

    A. Telecommunications Technology
        1. ~~Data transferred electronically~~ *Electronic data transfer*
        2. ~~Orders confirmed~~ *Confirmation of orders*
        3. ~~Shipping documents transmitted electronically~~
    B. Applications *(Current)*

3. Electronic transfer of shipping documents

(small organizations and   2

A bundle.

<u>Advantages</u>

Fiber optics have ~~many~~ *a number of* advantages. *Several* ~~Billions~~ bits per second can be transmitted ~~quickly~~. Thousands of these fibers can be packed in a single cable; thus, the cost of broadband transmission capability can be with in the reach of individuals in the future. A single fiber cable can carry *approximately* ~~about~~ 50,000 channels. Fiber-optic systems *are* ~~is~~ very reliable and stable. The bandwidth of these cables occupies (space less) than copper wire and eliminates line-of-sight problems. These systems are used to transmit data, *voice, or* ~~and~~ video. Some fiber-optic channels ~~are used~~ are not regulated by the Federal Communications Commission; consequently, frequency *allocation* does not develop into a problem. ~~It~~ In the next several years, *about* 30 per cent of the metropolitan transmission in the U. S. will be digital networks that are linked by optical-fiber cables.

<u>Additional Uses</u>

The use of optical fibers will *become increasingly* ~~be~~ prevalent in medicine, photoelectronics, military hardware, and photography. Bundles of optical fibers form part of gastriscopes and certain other medical instruments. These instruments *enable* ~~let~~ ~~medical~~ doctors to observe internal parts of the body without *conducting* surgery. The *expansion* ~~explanation~~ of these capabilities will bring about dramatic changes never thought possible in data communications.

(Surgical lasers *and instruments* for measuring temperature and/or pressure *also* will be using (fibers optical).

ELECTRONIC DATA INTERCHANGE IN THE TEXTILE INDUSTRY:

Market Technology Changing
New Information Technology

New information technology is bringing about ~~sweeping~~ *many* changes in the way domestic textile manufacturers are doing business. Point-of-sale terminals (POS) and electronic data interchange (EDI), a form of electronic mail,[1] have revolutionized the flow of information ~~in the industry.~~ Production managers are becoming aware of the new information available to them, ~~and they are applying this information to improve the efficiency of their operations.~~ *changes are coming rapidly, and those who wish to remain competitive are turning to telecommunications experts for advice.*

Producers of textiles have had to rely heavily on unscientific estimates of consumer demands. Predictions of future consumer trends were based on the opinions of style and fashion experts. If the experts were wrong, ~~however,~~ the negative impact on manufacturers with resources dedicated to producing unpopular goods was tremendous. As a result, the industry leaned towards a production-oriented mind-set. Emphasis was placed on large production runs (to reduce unit costs)[2] using readily available raw materials. If the produced goods *appeared to be* ~~were~~ unpopular with ~~the~~ consumers, then inventories backed up.

---

[1] "Electronic Mail, One Decade Old," The Wall Street Journal, 27 May 1987, p. 1.

[2] N. Allen Hunter, "How to Make Quick Response Work for You," Textile World (May 1986), pp. 54-55.

FIBER-OPTIC CABLES

Definition

Fiber-optic cables are changing traditional communication systems. The increased use of these cables allows enormous amounts of data to be transmitted at the speed of light through minute threads of glass or plastic (wires are not used). Lasers, which are light beams within a certain frequency range, are teamed with fiber optics to transmit the data.

Types

There are two types of fiber optics. Each type has a different construction, and each is used for different purposes.

Single-mode fibers. The first type of fiber optics is called single-mode fibers. They have small cores and only accept light along the axis of the fibers. They are used extensively for long-distance communication.

Multi-mode fibers. The second type is multi-mode fibers. These fibers have large cores, accept light from various angles, and are cheaper than single-mode fibers. Also, they are not used for long distances.

Technology

If the cylindrical surface of the fiber is not protected, light will be absorbed. For this reason, the fibers are coated with a low-refractive transparent material, such as glass or a special plastic. The coating thickness is of the order of the wavelength of light. This coating protects the total internal reflecting surface of the fiber and optically insulates adjacent fibers in

2

Considerable losses were incurred as markdowns were employed to move unwanted inventory.

In recent years, retailers have relied increasingly on electronic point-of-sale devices to record sales and control inventory levels. Information gathered daily from POS is used to prepare purchase orders and restock manufacturers' ~~store~~ shelves. ~~There are now enough POS terminals in retail stores across the country to act as the much-needed monitor of consumer demand.~~ Retailers are now receiving daily feedback about consumer preferences that used to take weeks or ~~even~~ months to collect.

Clothing producers are receiving this new consumer demand information in the form of purchase orders from retailers. In time, textile manufacturers will also feel the influence of the improved information flow as new orders are placed by their customers. Today's suppliers now find themselves in a consumer-oriented market.

~~Now~~ manufacturers are able to produce smaller and more marketable inventories that turn faster and require fewer markdowns. For example, Levi Strauss reported a drop in days of inventory from one month to a three-day supply after implementing EDI.[3] Lead times on production orders have shrunk from more than a month to less than a week in many ~~such manufacturing~~ cases. Traditional inventory costing systems failed as inventories began turning faster.

---

[3]David Wessel, "Computer Finds a Role in Buying and Selling, Reshaping Business," _The Wall Street Journal_, 16 October 1986, p. 1.

Closing.

following in alphabetical order, and the athletes ^of the host country enter^ last.

No ¶ After the Games are declared officially open by the president, ^or monarch^
of the host country, ~~an athlete~~ ^a runner^ enters the ~~arena~~ ^stadium^ and lights the
Ol~~y~~pic ^m^ flame with a torch that relays of runners have brought
from Olypia, ^Greece.^ This Flame continues to burn until the closing
ceremony, ^at which time it is extinguished.^

^There are victory ceremonies after each contest with the winners receiving a gold medal. At the closing ceremony, a ^each^ country
is represented by ^no more than^ six athletes, who march into the stadium again ~~and~~ ^but^
mingle without regard to nationality. ^Last, an^ ~~An~~ Olympic official declares
the games ~~ended~~ ^closed^ and invites the athletes to attend the next
Olympics. ^as a symbol of Olympic brotherhood.^

~~Games~~ ^Summer Games^

The Summer Games include 220 sports divided into ~~several~~ ^six primary^
categories: (1) athletic sports, (2) combative sports, (3) gymnastic
sports, (4) aquatic sports, (5) the modern pentathlon, and (6)
~~sports~~ equestrian ^sports.^ The modern pentathlon, usually contested by ~~the~~
military ^men^, includes horseback riding, fencing, shooting, swimming,
and cross-country running.

Winter Games

The Winter Games include ^only^ six ^official^ sports. Skating is divided into
speed ~~skating~~ and figure skating. Skiing is ^broken down^ ~~divided~~ into Alpine,
where contestants maneuver over a downhill course, and Nordic, which
includes cross-country ^and jumping events.^ ~~skiing with shooting.~~ The ~~luggage~~ ^luge^ involves
a small sled which attains speeds of over 160 miles ^per^ ~~an~~ hour. There
is competition in bobsledding and ~~in~~ ice hockey.

The biathlon combines cross-country skiing with rifle shooting.

3

EDI Concepts
~~Concept of Electronic Data Interchange~~

Manufacturers of textiles have been turning to EDI technology for answers. Just as POS terminals are used to gather information at the consumer level, EDI is the information system used at the retail and manufacturing levels. Studies show that approximately 70 percent of one computer's output is another computer's input, and 25 percent of transaction costs are caused by manual data entry.[4]

Telecommunications technology. EDI relies upon telecommunications technology to link the customer's computer directly to the supplier's computer. Once the computers are able to communicate, bottlenecks caused by conventional paper flows can be eliminated. Purchase orders are transmitted electronically to the supplier.

Current Applications. Current applications of EDI have been well received by both suppliers and their customers. ~~Customers~~ *Decision makers are concentrating on when the changes will take place and* ~~receive better service, and producers find that they are more~~ *how to make the transition to the new technology more* ~~competitive. Paper flow is reduced and information bottlenecks~~ *comfortable.*[5] ~~are eliminated,~~

[5] Glen Segal, "Information Processing Executes Quick Response," *Bobbin Magazine* (November 1986), pp. 72-76.

----

[4] McAllister Issacs, III, "Electronic Communication Cuts JIT Paperwork Flow," *Textile World* (December 1986), pp. 47-57.

OLYMPIC GAMES

<u>History</u>

The world's most important athletic events, attended by several million people and watched on television by hundreds of million more, are held every fourth year. The contests are divided into Summer Olympic Games, which are held in a major city; and Winter Olympic Games, which are held in a city or town in a mountainous, snow-covered area.

The Olympic Games began more than 2,700 years ago in Ancient Greece and ceased about 1,000 years later when Greek civilization declined. In 1896, they were revived and have grown steadily ever since. In 1900, in the Paris Games, women began competing; and in 1924, the Winter Olympic Games were held as a separate series. Because of World Wars I and II, no games were held in 1916, 1940, or 1944.

<u>Purposes</u>

There are two primary purposes of the Games:

1. To build individual character through athletic training.
2. To promote world peace among athletes of all nations.

<u>Ceremonies</u>

Whether summer or winter games, the Olympic Games open and close with great fanfare.

<u>Opening</u>. The Games open with a parade of all contestants who, dressed in their colorful uniforms, march into the stadium in national groups led by the athletes of Greece. The other nations

 If using a word processsior, recall JOB24. Then edit the bibliography using corrections shown below. If using a typewriter, key the bibliography from rough draft. Proofread and correct all errors.

- -

4

BIBLIOGRAPHY

"Electronic Mail, One Decade Old." <u>The Wall Street Journal</u>,
    27 May 1987, 1.

Hunter, N. Allen. "How to Make Quick Response Work for You."
    <u>Textile World</u> (May 1986), 54-55.

Issacs, McAllister, III. "Electronic Communication Cuts JIT
    Paperwork Flow." <u>Textile World</u> (December 1986), 47-57.

Wessel, David. "Computer Finds a Role in Buying and Selling,
    Reshaping Business." <u>The Wall Street Journal</u>, 16 October
    1986, 1.

Segal, Glen. "Information Processing Executes Quick Response." <u>Bobbin Magazine</u> (November 1986), 72-76.

- -

 If using word processor, recall JOB25. Then edit the title page, using information below. If using a typewriter, key the title page from the information shown below. Proofread and correct all errors.

Title: *TEXTILE INDUSTRY: ELECTRONIC DATA INTERCHANGE*

Name: *Robert Daniel Spillman*

School: *Walkertown Senior High School*

Date: *May 1, 19--*

- -

Reports for business and professional use are used by businesses to supply accurate and essential information. These business reports may be short and informal or longer and more complicated.

In Section A, you will key short, informal business reports. You will format both the simplified and traditional memorandums in Sections B and C. Sections D and E introduce more complicated business reports: documented business reports and professional journal articles. In the remaining sections, F and G, you learn how to prepare minutes of meetings and news releases. If you are using a word processor, use editing functions (see page 47).

Section A | SHORT, INFORMAL BUSINESS REPORTS

Most business decisions are based on reports. If reports are to be effective, they must be accurate, clear, and well organized.

The length of reports and the degree of their formality distinguish formal from informal reports. An informal report is short and has fewer parts. Short business reports do not usually include a title page, a contents page, or a reference list.

For convenience and simplicity, businesses use many types of short, informal reports. Some reports focus on day-to-day operations, while others deal with organizational change. Examples of short reports include a progress report, memo report, or a report within the body of a letter. A computer printout may also be considered a report.

1. Reports are usually DS, but they may be SS.
2. Margins: Top margin: first page, line 10 for pica and line 12 for elite; succeeding pages, line 8. Side margins: 1". Bottom margin: at least 1".
3. Page numbers: For second and following pages, type the page number on line 6 at right margin.
4. Main heading: Center in ALL CAPS; QS to body of report.
5. Side heading: Underline at left margin; initial cap main words; DS above and below side heading.
6. Paragraph heading: Indent 5 spaces and underline. Initial cap the first word of heading.
7. Quoted material: SS and indent 5 spaces from left margin.

DIFFERENTIAL ELECTRICAL RATES REPORT   line 12, elite
line 10, pica

QS

Background

    If one accepts the "embedded cost" or "cost-of-service" methodology of rate setting, differential prices for residential, industrial, and commercial customers are justified. Differential rates are not justified for the following two points:

    1. Electricity rates should be based on the marginal cost of electricity production and distribution.

    2. Marginal cost of electricity is the same for all customers.

    Marginal cost. By way of amplification, the marginal cost differs at different times of the day. Also, there is justification for charging different customers different rates. Differentials in billing expenses should be reflected in a customer's charge. The customer's charge should also be based on marginal costs: the marginal cost of attaching a customer to the existing power system and the marginal cost associated with servicing that customer. Both marginal costs are independent of the amount of electricity used.

    Embedded cost. To those who have not devoted some thought to the issues of prices and costs in a market economy, the "embedded-cost" methodology purports to equate the total expenditures of each class with the total cost of serving that class. The methodology has been used for many years to determine rates, not only for the electric power industry, but for all regulated utilities. We now know that this methodology is wrong. Rate-making, like other human activity, is subject to progress. Dividing electrical consumers

(at least 1")

2

into classes reflects a time when life was less complicated. Variations from accepted routines were practically nonexistent. In today's society, there is no norm; it is the age of the individual.

Marginal Cost Pricing

    The price which a customer pays for electricity affects the amount of electricity which is consumed. Prices act as a signal. To insure that consumption is efficient, prices should reflect the true cost of serving that customer. Although present electric rates purport to do this, they do not. A residential customer's rate is based upon the behavior of all residential customers. However, a customer has no control over the behavior of all residential customers. The division of customers into the present three classes makes no more sense than dividing customers according to their race, their hair color, or some other characteristic over which they have no control.

    Cost conditions. The rates charged a customer should be based upon the costs which the customer imposes on the utility, not the costs of some "class." An ideal rate structure should meet the following conditions: DS

    If any customer decides to increase power consumption, the increase in the bill should equal, as closely as possible, the extra cost the power companies must bear to supply that additional power. Similarly, if any customer decides to decrease power consumption, the reduction in the bill should equal, as closely as possible, the reduced cost to the power companies. DS

    These conditions could be met by marginal cost pricing; they are not met by the current price structure.

Proofreader's Marks

═ or ‖	Align type
Cap or ☰	Capitalize
lc or /	Use lowercase
⌒	Close up horizontal space
⟨	Close up vertical space
#	Insert horizontal space
>	Insert vertical space
℘	Delete or omit
∪ or tr	Transpose
∧	Insert copy shown
∨	Insert apostrophe
⋏	Insert comma
⊙	Insert period
⦂	Insert colon
∨ ∨	Insert quotation marks
⨀	Insert semicolon
stet	Let it stand; ignore the correction
sp	Spell out
SS	Single-space
DS	Double-space
QS	Quadruple-space
___	Underline or italicize
⊏	Move left
⊐	Move right
¶	Paragraph
no new ¶	No new paragraph
≡	All CAPS

Editing Functions

bold - used to darken a word or block of text for emphasis within a document

center - used to automatically center text between the left and right margins

copy - used to duplicate a portion of text. The text will remain in its original position as well as appear in another section of the document.

define - used to isolate a block of text in order to move, copy, or delete it

delete - used to remove a space or text in a document

find - used to automatically locate a word or words in a document

footnotes - used to enter a superscript footnote number in text and in references at the bottom of the page

go to - used to automatically get to a specific page, character, or word within a document

headers/footers - used to print text at the top (header) or bottom (footer) of the pages within a document

home/end - used to automatically go to the beginning (home) or end (end) of the page or document

insert/replace - used to either add text (insert) or key text over existing text (replace) within a document

justify text - used to align text at the left margin (usually the default), the right margin (right justification or justify), or (half justify) to create a more even right margin than the normal left justification

merge - used normally to add variables to a form letter. This allows you to add one document to another document.

move - used to take a block of text and move it to another section of the document

overstrike - used to mark over existing text using a different character. This allows you to see changes made to the document.

pagination - used to decide where to end pages of a document. This can be done manually, automatically, or using both manual and automatic pagination.

paragraph indent (aligned) - used to automatically set up paragraphs so they are aligned at the left and/or right margins of a document

recall - used to retrieve a document or block of text

save - used to save (store) a document so you can later revise or print it

search/replace - used to automatically find a word or words and replace with other text

spell check - used to scan your document for misspelled or unfamiliar words

superior numbers - used to create a superscript number in the text or in footnotes

tab - used to set specific tab positions within a document

underscore (underline) - used to underline text within a document